Letters to a
Young Activist

Also by Todd Gitlin

*Media Unlimited: How the Torrent of Images
and Sounds Overwhelms Our Lives*

Sacrifice

*The Twilight of Common Dreams: Why America Is
Wracked by Culture Wars*

The Murder of Albert Einstein

The Sixties: Years of Hope, Days of Rage

Watching Television (editor)

Inside Prime Time

*The Whole World Is Watching: Mass Media in the
Making and Unmaking of the New Left*

Busy Being Born

*Campfires of the Resistance: Poetry from the
Movement* (editor)

Uptown: Poor Whites in Chicago (coauthor)

Todd Gitlin

letters to a
young activist

BASIC
BOOKS

A Member of the Perseus Books Group
New York

Published by Basic Books,
A Member of the Perseus Books Group

Designed by Rick Pracher
Set in 11-point Janson Text by the Perseus Books Group

Library of Congress Cataloging-in-Publication Data
Gitlin, Todd.
    Letters to a young activist / Todd Gitlin.
        p. cm.
    Includes bibliographical references.
    ISBN 0-465-02738-5 (alk. paper)
    1. Political activists. 2. Political participation. 3. Social
movements.   I. Title.

JF799 .G57 2003
322.4—dc21   2002152385

03 04 05 / 10 9 8 7 6 5 4 3 2 1

To three who don't quit:
Anthony Barnett, Nissim Calderon and
Robert Jay Lifton

And in memory of Paul Wellstone,
who never quit either

Contents

Letters to a
Young Activist

1

On Duty, Love and Adventure, or Some Leaps of Faith

Dear ——,

Let's agree to overlook (maybe even enjoy) the absurdity that joins us: You agree to indulge my lecturing on matters I didn't quite understand until I was older than you, and I make every effort to connect to your passions and objections—to take your arguments seriously, even though you're too young to have had the experience I draw on. Fine. We need each other. Let's both try to think our way out of our skins.

To start out, let's recognize that it's hard to be honest about age—as hard as it is necessary. Here is Max Weber in his great lecture of 1918, "Politics as a Vocation": "The mere fact that someone is twenty years of age and that I am over fifty is no cause for me to think that this alone is an achievement before which I am overawed. Age is not decisive; what is decisive is the trained relentlessness in viewing the realities of life, and the ability to

face such realities and to measure up to them inwardly."
When I was twenty and read these words for the first
time, they didn't make much of an impression. (So much
the worse for me, and no excuse for you.) Nonetheless,
that we aren't the first to face our quandaries and tasks is
some comfort.

So: You invite me to investigate what I've learned on
a subject that isn't normally—either in media or the
academy—considered much of a subject. What I offer
in these letters isn't a declaration of how things are or a
precise political outlook or social analysis or a set of positions (except when I can't resist) or moral philosophy
or history or memoir or a critique of other books. Instead, I'll ruminate on experience and principles of action. I may reminisce now and again, not to usher back
the Wonder Years with a sepia glow but to put some life
behind my arguments. Though I address mainly liberals, the Left and left of center, in these letters I try not
to convey a political manifesto or a rally of nerve and
verve but a sense of activism's proper spirit. I want to
approach some of the big questions about the activist
spirit and how it ought to play out in the world. The
questions I *won't* address very much are, What world
should I want? and Why is the world as it is? What I
hope to address (and testify to) is, *How should I think
about what to do?* I will draw on a strange kind of knowledge that lacks the pleasing *click* of a theoretical box well
constructed. This isn't book learning; it doesn't follow
from theory. This knowledge is plainer, more homely,
more practical, I hope (you be the judge), more useful
and, I think, more true. Yet it is neither career counsel
nor self-help.

What follows is meant to convey what I have come to think (*concluded* would probably be premature) in the course of trying to change the world. In many ways— sometimes more grandiose, at times more modest—this has rarely been far from my mind and feelings, even in times of despair, disgust and withdrawal, since the day in 1960 when I found myself at a rally against nuclear bombs in Boston. With some sense of wonderment I soon started going to meetings, trying to figure out what I thought, debating, fretting, campaigning for candidates, knocking on doors, joining and organizing demonstrations, circulating petitions, writing letters to politicians and bureaucrats, piecing together leaflets and press releases and horrifying my parents—an *activist*, though we didn't use the word then. This was my world in the sixties—in what we called *the movement*—a force that wasn't just the sum of all civil rights, antiwar, anti-apartheid (and so forth) demonstrations we played out in public but also the private lives we lived out accordingly. Outsiders called us *protesters*, but protest was only one of our faces. We were trying to build—or be—a better so-ciety. The idea of the movement erased the distinction between public and private; as a way of life, it was a net-work of linkages, public bonds that were so private as to erase this distinction—a dangerous idea, actually, but I'll get to that later. Everyone I knew well for more than a decade lived in the movement.

The movement emphasized two things: collectivity and animation. By contrast, in this mainly antipolitical era, the label of choice is *activist*—and it's poignant (though not altogether sad) that today we address re-cruits mainly one at a time, not *as* a movement. They don't clump. I don't remember hearing this ungainly word *activist* until the mid seventies. I had gone back to graduate school where I read through scholarly articles to see whether they made any sense of the whirlwind I had been through. There we were, an object of study: *activists*. I thought the term denatured, uncomprehending and evasive: a category label for the convenience of investigators. In the early New Left, we preferred *organizer*: someone who moves people into action and doesn't just rouse them for a particular occasion, who doesn't come and go but steadily works up strategies, focuses energies and (crucially) settles in for the long haul. Europeans speak of *militants*, meaning more or less the reliables. Now people talk of *social entrepreneurs*—those who launch projects, construct organizations; these are social artists, in a sense, who create something new in the world.

One other thing that seems wrong with the term *activist* turns out to be illuminating. *Activist* sounds misleading because of that profligate little syllable *-ist* that implies belief about how things are and ought to be: social*ist*, fasc*ist*, femin*ist*, environmental*ist*, Islam*ist*, what have you. An activist is a different sort of *-ist*, for it's not your beliefs that make you one but your beliefs hooking up to your activities. An activist refuses to take the world for granted. Faced with pain and evil, the activist is not content to deplore or rage or regret, does not just believe or wish or declare but thinks: I'm not an outsider to the world, and the world—with all its persecutions, endangerments and wonders—is not an outsider to me. History is not (or not only) something that other people do. My action and yours are the heart of the matter. If we act wisely, we become more than ourselves: artisans of the good. So *activist*, though not a lovely word, is a useful one because it reminds us that the world not only *is* but is *made*: Human beings make history, though as a brilliant but monomaniacal prophet once wrote, not in conditions of their own making—and, I would add, not always with the results they prefer, to put it mildly.

Suffering is a human condition. So is the desire to act against a sea of sorrows. I'm supposing that you're reading this book because you've already decided you want to do something useful against the crimes and sins, the starvation and massacre, torture and terror, ecological damage, disease, bigotry, the suppression of castes (women and racial groups among them), a whole multitude of oppressions. In the activist camp, you join a tradition both illustrious and indispensable, one with many successes to point to: against slavery, brutal working conditions, colonial conquest, unjust war, the humiliation of women and sexual minorities, racial discrimination and class degradation, the despoliation of nature—and toward liberty, equality, fraternity and the right to pursue happiness, not to mention beautiful peace and a livable planet.

Where would the world be without agitators? Great ideals wouldn't stand a chance. Radiant goals that conservatives say they hope to conserve are not and cannot be achieved by conservatives. The Confederacy would not have abolished slavery. The eight-hour day, the minimum wage, Social Security, public funding for medical care and higher education, clean water, rain forests and species preserved were not dreamed up by corporations or status quo governments. The federal bureaucracy and pharmaceutical companies did not put anti-AIDS drugs into the hands of millions of infected people out of good will, without a raging activist movement. It's obvious when you think about it but neglected in the conservatives' self-congratulation: without the disrupters, campaigners and ideological pests, all noble words amount to nothing but blackboard dust. This is not to justify every activity undertaken in the name of activism but to state a plain historical truth: no noise, no improvement. Activism as such is not sufficient for improvement, but damned if it isn't necessary.

So for joining the activist camp in the face of an immensity of pain and crime, congratulations and thank you. You've departed from the path of least resistance—a clue to good character and the promise of a life well spent. You have the nerve to face reality in a culture that, every day, hands out innumerable good-timey means of evasion. Facing the world's travails, you aren't content to stop at taking notice or bearing witness. You aren't satisfied to deplore, weep or yell. Your response to the day's bad news is not, Isn't that awful? but What am I—what are *we*—going to do about that?

I'm tempted to write—in the spirit of the resonant commencement address—that never before has activism been more necessary, and this might even be true. Later, I'll have something to say about the unprecedented size and scale of today's dangers. Yet given the vast amount of unnecessary suffering in the world, the important existential truth is that anytime is a good time to try to change the world. Perhaps it is too late to save humanity from the damages already suffered and done, but it is never too late to see about making the future more tolerable. You're indignant that misery should be the common lot of billions of people, and you're not one for close calculations of the percentages of lives at risk, because complacency and rationalization aren't your game. You don't want to put up with suffering that might, after all, be helped.

Your longing for a better, more just world requires neither apology nor excuse. It is not a sign of geekiness or unhipness. To face reality is only realism—real war, real racism, real ruination, starvation and all the rest—whatever others may think, know or feel. You've discovered that activity brings exuberance and you rightly suspect anyone who passes off your pleasure as a neurotic symptom, a flight from your proper private pursuits, a drying up of your own well of happiness, a hand-me-down from your parents or some other accident of existence. Refusing to feel at home in a world of stupendous inequality is nothing to be ashamed of. Cambodian children can look forward to living 47 years in full health, and children in Sierra Leone (where 28 percent die before their fifth birthday), 29.5 years. An American can expect 67.3 years, and a Japanese 73.8 years—not to mention the inequalities *within* each country. That Planet Earth is filling up with instruments of mass destruction, that they can even roar out of a splendid blue sky in your neighborhood, should be taken seriously. This potential is not just a feature of the world since September 11, 2001, it has become a standing feature of the world as we know it and as our successors will know it. Let anyone call you a loser (pettiest of American insults) for feeling that your cursed spite is to set the world right: You can reply that this is how you affirm membership in the human race. Besides, you're forging a way of life full of pleasures and even marvels, not least the thrill of bending history, pulling it your way.

How large is the portion of suffering that might be helped? You don't know the limits. (Neither do I.) But resist the temptation to think you are ushering in an earthly paradise. Also resist the conservative lowball— the cynicism that relishes prophecies such as "The poor shall ye always have with ye" as reasons to turn your back on the impoverished here and now (whether in Afghanistan or down the street). If perfection is precluded from human affairs, as antiutopians remind you, don't take that as an excuse for inaction. Without your activity, things might well be worse. Have the courage to toss away illusion, which is a crutch. Be willing to take the chance that you might leave the world better than you found it—though without any guarantees. You don't need guarantees.

Activism does not presuppose fairy-tale knowledge of happy or unhappy endings. No certitude exists except in fundamentalist ranks. Beware them: Apocalyptics are both dangerous and lazy. To predicate your actions on some assurance of vindication—because history or God is on your side, and socialism or anarchism or for that matter corporate capitalism or what have you is the preordained endpoint for human destiny—is to surrender your finite human nature to historical opportunism. Needing to bet on the right horse is a human weakness you're better off without. A happy-ending cosmology is feel-good stuff, like many another fancy or fantasy, but the truth is that you must act in suspension, neither

not means—ends

clairvoyant nor fatalistic. You'll organize unions, support sweatshop workers, push for a living wage, oppose unjust wars and violence against women—all because it's honorable to try, not because you're bound to prevail. Outcomes are opaque. Just as history does not end, neither therefore does the need to repair, reform and go on reforming. The need for activism will not go out of style—though earlier activist fashions will, and should.

So you need a sense of irony, not the sarcasm that masquerades as intelligent distance—the fatalist's smirk, the brainless, all-corrosive knowing derision alleged to have gone out of fashion on September 11—but the dark recognition that in history, as in love, you can't always get what you want. History does not proceed in a straight line but rather in zigzags, reversals, arabesques, curlicues, even pleasant surprises. (The cold war ends—great news. Genocide ensues and Islamist terrorism revs up—terrible news.) Then take a cue from the Mick Jagger School of Hard Knocks: You need not be paralyzed by the recognition that you *can't* always get what you want. A tragic sense of irony is not the same as despair, a rolling of eyes or a Bronx cheer. To be resolute is to face the reality that the fight at hand may fail—at least partly—but no defeat is definitive. You rethink. The world changes and you rethink again. You're never finished.

A symbolic footnote to the Jagger theory of modesty is the Chicken Little story told by Daniel Ellsberg. Chicken Little is thrashing around on the floor, flapping her wings wildly, clucking and shouting, "The sky is falling! The sky is falling!" "Why are you going on like that?" asks Ducky Lucky, reasonably enough. "How is flapping your wings and clucking going to help?" Says Chicken Little, "You do what you can." If Chicken Little were more logical, she might add, "Anyway, flapping and clucking can't hurt. And if you're so smart, how is *not* flapping and *not* clucking going to help?"

So activism is a leap of faith—but not into a void. The activist works toward improvement, not salvation. A doctor does not treat the sick in the belief that no one will ever again fall sick. In truth, everyone will fall sick. Medicine is simply humanity's gift to itself, a gift of betterment, a way of life. You will never be satisfied—and so be it. Your pride is in your efforts, the seriousness and intelligence with which you take your dilemmas, and the vitality with which you live them. Even a connoisseur of lost causes does not know with certainty that the next will also be lost.

You do what you can—and in the right spirit. The wrong motives not only corrupt and betray you, they are more likely to bring bad results. The three great motives are duty, love and adventure.

Of duty, you'd think not much needs to be said, yet we are so far from a shared notion of duty in this era that just after September 11, 2001, President George W. Bush told Americans their duty was to fly to Disney World and spend money. The very word *duty* has an obsolete ring, like a blacksmith shop. The classic poster enshrining duty, Uncle Sam pointing his finger under the slogan "I Want You," is retro, a collectible item long out of style. In the present day, even the armed forces seem embarrassed by duty—never mind that we are supposed to be at war. After the Vietnam War corrupted the idea of conscription, the U.S. Army started recruiting with the career-building slogan "Be All That You Can Be." In 2001, they replaced that with the higher-tech self-sufficiency slogan "An Army of One." Self-fulfillment is the balm of our time; duty is archaic.

You, however, may feel like a refugee from an acquisitive society wrapped in a fun culture that despises duty. Duty presupposes others outside yourself who are equally worthy, others on whom you depend (and who depend on you) not only for livelihood but for safety, esteem and, paradoxically, your own freedom. Not for you the usual obsessions with getting (money and kicks), spending (money, especially on kicks), borrowing (money for kicks), betting (ditto), and following (stars, teams, drugs and other novelties *du jour*). Conventional thrills leave you insufficiently thrilled. You take responsibility for the tone and worthiness of your society, and you are embarrassed by what you behold. If that weren't enough, you take responsibility for the fate of the earth. You're aware that you're indebted to predecessors who refused to live for their isolated selves alone. Your moment in time was bequeathed by their moments in time. Battles they lost are still inspirations. Battles they won for equal rights, decent working and living conditions, treaties against war and genocide, put a floor under you. The struggle against sweatshops in early twentieth-century America made your struggles against sweatshops in Asia (and yes, still North America) possible.

Your duty derives from love—but be careful lest your rhetoric of love disguise its diabolical distant relation, hatred. You must be willing to go deeply into yourself, plunge into philosophical and psychological thickets and ask, Do I really love whom I claim to love, or do I only claim to love them to justify an abhorrence or a political program? How can I be sure? Don't try to wriggle away from these problems. They're problems for good reason. What is ostensibly love's benign gaze can turn out to mask a deeper hate—and the difference may not be easy to detect. (More on this in Letter 4.) You may lie to yourself. Your true skill may lie on the side of hate. You may indulge the romantic, antibourgeois tradition—the West's selective love of the non-West, the love of the rich for the poor, or the love of the established for the pariah, about whom, frequently, all that's known is that they hate people like you. You may recruit as friends abstractions of whom you have little or no direct knowledge. All you really know is that you share an enemy. Such brittle love most likely is no love at all, only a rationalization for hate; it partakes of all the problems with hate, which I'll get to in my next letter.

The other problem with love as a motive is, Who will be left out of your circle of love, and what will you do about them? Many are the crimes committed in the name of love—crimes of war, in fact. Love of your own, of people like yourself, people with whom you share an identity (or more precisely, people with whom you decide to share an identity and overlook differences) slides easily into what Erik Erikson called *pseudospeciation*—the belief that your tribe, clan, family, class, race, nation, ethnicity, religion is the whole of humanity. What you undertake in their name therefore overrides limits. This is a vast and consequential blindness. You must also dissolve sentimentality, learn to criticize and disappoint those whom you love. (I had to work to get my mind around the fact that civil rights veterans such as Stokely Carmichael, an admirable figure for years in the sixties, might later delude themselves that Israel is the root of Africa's misery. I also had to learn early that Jews are not automatically lovers of justice—Professor Henry Kissinger taught that lesson well with his loose talk about "limited nuclear war." I later had to learn as well that just because my parents suspected anti-Semitism from many quarters and I was in revolt against my parents, they were still, often enough, right.) Love of your own veers easily into race hatred, religious hatred, national hatred—some of the ugliest passions known.

Perhaps nothing can save you from either anguish or error. No matter. *Bring on the future!* you say, secure in the knowledge that it is plunging toward us like it or not; but you would find it ignoble to accept the inevitability of defeat. You are not averse to long odds, but to shrug, cringe or whine in the face of them would be demeaning. You don't have to be a smiley-face optimist to consider that since you can't really know enough to know what the future brings, you might as well stay open to bright possibilities. Openness is one of your virtues, built into your kind of practical intelligence. The activist spirit saves you from dourness, coldness, desperation— from the habit-forming victim mentality in all its self-fulfilling dread. You're always looking for opportunities. Fortitude works in your favor, but another quality of the activist spirit leavens your fortitude, makes it humanly bearable and even better, attractive. This is the taste for adventure, which I think must be a quality of your being.

Yes, the fact that you're adventuresome is one thing I know about you. You refuse to take the world or yourself for granted. You don't think the future is doomed to replay the past. You're an empiricist, not an ideologue—you're open to new fact, even about who you might turn out to be once you take some personal chances. Yet the usual adventures strike you as stale, scripted and petty. You know there must be more to life than going to concerts, eating in restaurants, dosing yourself with sensational substances, trying out fabulous sports and working in unexciting jobs that enable you to afford the aforementioned pleasures. Others will consider it odd that in a society that offers so many adventures at such affordable rates, you should have chosen something so unusual as organizing a union or campaigning against war crimes or working for human rights or environmental justice. But the oddity of your pursuit in your eyes is no disqualification—it's a measure of how cramped is the public imagination. You don't mind being countercyclical. You even relish it—though not in the persnickety sense of the contrarian, who predictably follows orders but in reverse: He is enslaved to *No*, rebelling for the sake of rebellion. Contrarianism is a perverse submission to power. It refuses initiative. Playfulness, though, pursues action, not reaction.

In other words, when you act politically, act playfully too—not out of sheer contrariness but out of free delight. Duty requires reason—because you don't want your action to interfere with your goals—but duty is not condemned to bleakness. Duty leaves room for joyful initiative. Just because you let the dark side of the world into your nervous system doesn't mean that you have to surrender to gloom, which in any case is never as justified as it thinks. Let the poseurs sneer at the activists, calling them humorless while wearing humorless smirks—they don't know what they're missing. Playfulness also has another meaning: It is openness to experience, and openness to experience is how we learn. I think of many moments of joyful self-education in the 1960s—the all-night conversational highs of the Free Speech Movement in Berkeley, the wild and sometimes reckless hijinks of the underground press, many comic Yippie moments (like Abbie Hoffman and Jerry Rubin raining dollar bills on the floor of the New York Stock Exchange, gloating at the pile-on that greed incites). Imagine the situationist graffiti of Paris—"Beneath the pavement, the beach." "All power to the imagination!" "The more I make love, the more I make revolution" (and vice versa). Imagine! Human beings in modern times made a carnival of life. They were not embarrassed by a surfeit of joy.

Joy's great escort is originality. You never know when you're creating a precedent. Let me single out a less heralded moment from my own experience. In 1965, I helped Students for a Democratic Society (SDS) organize a sit-in at the headquarters of the Chase Manhattan Bank in downtown Manhattan, to protest loans to the government of South Africa. With such loans, a consortium of American banks had helped bail out the apartheid regime after the massacre of sixty-nine unarmed black Africans at Sharpeville in 1960. Our point was simple: Banking as usual in lower Manhattan had blood written all over it. We printed up buttons: CHASE MANHATTAN, PARTNER IN APARTHEID. Vindication was ours when the bank went to court seeking an injunction banning the distribution of our buttons and leaflets making our argument—suddenly freedom of speech was not an abstraction. On March 19, forty-one of us sat down on the sidewalk outside the bank and got ourselves carried off in a paddy wagon. We didn't get much media and we didn't care.

Today, demonstrators at the World Bank and International Monetary Fund sometimes pursue an equivalent happiness. After the March 1965 sit-in, SDS moved into anti–Vietnam War activity, but the Congress of Racial Equality, various mainline church groups and the American Committee on Africa continued these projects for years. In the mid 1980s, the spirit of these actions revived. A broad movement sprang up to divest university funds from companies invested in South Africa. Divestment became a popular cause, taken up at enough universities (and cities, churches and elsewhere) to hurt the racist regime. The movement built up pressure to release Nelson Mandela and legitimize the African National Congress. The campaign was a tributary into the great current that washed away apartheid in South Africa. On the grand scale of history, our demonstration was a tiny event—trivial, even—but joyous. We dressed duty up for a party.

So did the Seattle demonstrators of 1999, many thousands of them, the Teamsters marching with Greens dressed as sea turtles, greatly outnumbering the Starbucks window smashers (as if the news media cared).

The worth of such moments is not canceled out by their evanescence. All moments, all joys prove evanescent. Those of dour disposition always threaten to take over. And so?

Be original. See what happens.

2
On the Burden of History, or Several Warped Ways of Looking at the Sixties

Dear ——,

A sticky subject stands between us: the quagmire sixties. Doesn't the subject massively irritate you? Your heart (like mine) sinks at the pop-up clichés that substitute for historical sense in a culture that despises "been there done that." Then again, sometimes you're awed, dazzled by the romance, convinced that if you don't live up to your predecessors, you're nothing. My generation had its own version of that: the myth of the magnificent French resistance, which turns out to have been rather punier than we imagined. We all rummage around for forebears, lest we feel utterly marooned in history. But all such mystiques, whatever their share of truth, become distortions by the time they get into popular circulation. Consider the recent "greatest generation" effusions, rightly honoring the Americans who fought World War II but wholly uninterested in the appeasement pursued by many of that same generation's leaders, fostering fascism and bringing on World War II in the first place.

One way or the other, I know you're burdened by the weight of the sixties—at least the glamorous or lurid versions that drift through the media and popular memory. (Who programs the media, after all, but baby boomers?) More than once, when the subject comes up in conversations with younger activists, beneath a certain fascination I've heard an undercurrent of weak groans: *There you guys go again. . . . Boomer bravado. . . . War stories. . . . Golden oldies. . . . You guys not only had the moral clarity of a fight against evil (Vietnam, white supremacy), you had all the fun and left us with AIDS, Republicans, and rock 'n' roll jingles for SUVs. . . .*

No, I don't blame you a bit if you're sick and tired of hearing about our glory days. Who wouldn't feel burdened by having to conduct your life as an aftermath? Your actions are shadowed, measured, invidiously or not, accurately or not, against the luminous era when putative giants walked the earth. Whatever you do, the gatekeepers of the press seek out learned experts such as yours truly to comment sagely, or at least quotably, on how your actions do and don't resemble those of yore. (The journalists are usually old enough that the sixties formed their bedrock sense of what young rebels are like—and of course they view their own youth with requisite fondness.) How can you not feel preempted, diminished—even by your parents and teachers sitting around the proverbial campfire retelling (not for the first time) their antiwar stories? The afterglow threatens to steal your sense of uniqueness—an especially bracing propensity in a land that relishes the feeling of getting born again at the drop of an advertising campaign. Nothing you can do about your date of birth, after all. So you're trapped. The sixties (like parents) are useful but also oppressive. What would you do without them? What can you do with them?

I can't tell you it isn't thrilling to take center stage— not only to "put your body on the line," as the civil rights movement told us, but to watch the authorities re- act to you, to celebrate the almost sinful pleasure of be- ing right, to see people surge into your ranks, to feel that your analysis penetrates to the heart of things. The lore isn't wrong: The sixties *were* thrilling. That's one reason why we grizzled types get a hazy look in our eyes when we reminisce. It's not just that we're trying to remember, or to forget. Never mind all the ironical defenses we've fashioned to protect ourselves from the burning flares of hope that we once harbored in a past too far gone to re- trieve but for little shards of memory. Look at the miser- able state of the world! Why shouldn't we feel pained at the yawning gap between the grandest ideals of our youth and the bitter world we actually live in?

But the thrill was more thrill than you know—more and different than you've been encouraged to know. The real badge of belonging wasn't bell-bottoms, tie-dyes and the Beatles; it was joy that came from the sense of movement. Not the herd instinct—we were, each of us, too strong-willed for that—but vitality and conviviality together, a feeling of overcoming drift in favor of mas- tery. It was comradeship—the feeling of trust. We called it love, which meant it was more than an idea.

The deepest thrills came about because some cre- ative souls found some thrilling potential in moments that left others cold. In a word, they *invented*. Invention is what's decisive, not a birth certificate. There's no wrong time to live, only the right way to live *your* one and only life at the moment you're living it. There's always the need to think through what is new, maybe unprecedented, in the situation you face—always the need to devise the tactics that make sense in your milieu. There's always the need to confront—which doesn't mean shout down—your adversaries' arguments. And to withstand the seen-it-all, know-it-all sneers of your elders (even this one), but with arguments, not sneers of your own.

Newness is invigorating—always a gift to the young, implying a freedom that is as delicious as it is unsolicited. At the time, we were audacious enough to think (for a while) that we were devising a *New* Left, but we didn't invent this expectation, either. Americans like it—and not only Americans. Jean-Paul Sartre put it beautifully writing about his own school crowd: "We thought the world was new because we were new in the world." (He was writing about the twenties.) So it's a blow to your collective egotism—a quality for which I am not singling you out—to be juxtaposed automatically to yesteryear, reminded that the world was not born yesterday (nor were your ideas).

I hear you revel in your break from the past. The sense of discontinuity can be bracing. My crowd in SDS used to love trashing "the old farts" of the parent organization—too stodgy, too stuck on labor, too obsessed with their anticommunism. We came to think that we suffered in some ways because there was a "missing generation" on the Left, more or less a decade older than us—older brothers and sisters, in a sense. We felt marooned. Yet on the whole, we actually benefited, because the stolid, dogma-dosed, Stalin-tainted and Stalin-haunted elder generation had been crushed by the twin pincers of McCarthyism and its own inner fatuousness by the time we came along. The collapse of American communism under the double pressure of McCarthyism and Khrushchev's revelations of (some) Stalinist crimes in 1956 produced a mixed blessing as well as a curse. The curse is obvious: When we came along, McCarthy's political career was over but his *ism* was still intimidating cautious people. When garden-variety Americans were afraid to sign petitions, fearing that a Big Brother government would frown, the chill on *all* left-wing political expression was palpable. But such is the cunning of history that the demise of the Old Left also had the effect of clearing the way for a fresh—democratic, searching, pragmatic—New Left that for a time offered vastly more promise than any replenished Old Left could have done. Had American communism been more vigorous in the early 1960s, it might well have tied the new movements in knots, tethering the early New Left to morally and intellectually bankrupt positions or the endless fight against them. The New Left would not have been able to be as new as it was (for a while).

So our sixties movement had the luck of historical isolation. We felt free to invent ourselves. (Arguably, too free.) During our formative years, our tactical and rhetorical moves were rarely smothered by elders, by the press, by residues of the thirties. We were not weighed down by the sense of coming too late. We were not subjected over and over again to comparisons. Political campaigns of the sixties were not weighed down by claims and counterclaims about what candidate X or Y had been up to in the thirties. In the main, the thirties (including their good side, the tradition of trade union militancy) had been tipped into a black hole of oblivion. In the early sixties, we were relatively unfazed by sectarian left-wing relics controlling our organizations and turning them into front groups, passing out their shrieking, jargonized newspapers at our demonstrations, declaiming their warmed-over spiels about The Road to Revolution at our meetings. They were around, but little more than a nuisance. For a few years we were able to be a New Left—to try, anyway—because the Old Left was almost completely defunct. Later came infiltrations. When, in 1965–1966, Stalinist remnants (mainly the Progressive Labor Party) caught on to the fact that burgeoning SDS was a happy hunting ground for recruiting (boring from within *in every sense*)—when SDS was unfortified to withstand them (we were naïve enough to think that excluding people who disagreed with us was "red-baiting") or thought the way to defeat them was to become truer Marxists (or eventually, truer Marxist-Leninists)—that was the beginning of the end of genuinely *new* Left thinking.

Today you can't turn around without bumping into the sixties, its oldies but goodies, its scraps, as if the essential history of activism has already been engraved in the books but for footnotes. Whereas relics of the thirties had just about been purged from popular culture by the time the sixties dawned, relics of the sixties are today everywhere—in music, cartoons, movies, slogans, logos, hairstyles, mechanically tie-dyed T-shirts, Woodstock revivals, you name it. Everything in American culture turns into a theme park, every stretch of time gets packaged as a stylistic decade, so why should the sixties, rich in recyclable relics, be any different? And this is one reason why you are required at times to work hard at dispelling the sense of coming too late.

So I'm not blind to your problem. The sixties truly were amazing, one after another annus mirabilis and annus horribilis superimposed on each other. We had scale and momentum. (Consider 1968 alone, with convulsions in Vietnam, Columbia, Paris, Prague, Chicago and Mexico City.) All these explosions of hope and grand possibility, all the confrontations and evils, all the assassinations, riots, political trials and other disasters, all the mental and social experiments—news of it all speedily amplified (and often enough warped) by television, which thought it knew a big story when it saw one and was often right. When we plunge into the quagmire of the far gone but ever-golden sixties, though, we see not only that those times were probably not what you think—not what you have been led to think—but also that what follows from the force and scale of the movements is not exactly clear.

You may have assumed that in the sixties radicalism was all the rage. Everyone—everyone who mattered, that is—was doing the latest step. Poor you, born too late for all the excitement. Today, despite the big kickoff for a movement against war in Iraq, discouragement may prompt the question, Why bother? At the far end of this reasoning, there may well be times when you yourself, not just your inactivist friends, take the sixties legend as a rationale for immobility. Why bother taking action when the time's not ripe, when all the great deeds have already been done? Fatalism is a meek rebellion against actual or symbolic parents. The assumption that radicalism was all the rage easily curdles into a self-protective moan. You may have friends who shrug that little or nothing is to be done now because "there's no movement"—forgetting that one reason there's no movement is that most everyone who would make a movement thinks there's no movement and therefore neglects to make one. As if the movement of the sixties sprang full-blown from a New Year's Eve celebration when we sang good-bye to Ike and hello to JFK. This can't be said too often: movements are made, not born.

There's also the oversimplified legend that the sixties movement was bound to win and therefore we were giddy with hope—a sort of Pepsi generation, effervescent with goodness, destined to have it all, from easy contraception to moral grandeur. We are supposed to have been lucky enough to have capitalized on our grand demographics (thus, the common confusion of sixties movements with the much larger but absurdly vague category of "baby boomers"). In collective memory—a sloppy hodgepodge of lore, bad TV movies, pop-musical roundups and pundit formulas—the New Left, civil rights and antiwar movements are assumed to have developed smoothly because we were in tune (so it's said) with the generational zeitgeist, as if on January 1, 1960, everybody who was alive from the neck up (or the waist down) woke up and crowed, "Hey, gang, it's time to do *the sixties*. All together now." This view is not only self-serving, it's false.

Factually, on the question of how the terrain looked, in 1960, 1961, 1962, a lot of the smart money predicted a conservative future. My college class, '63, was on the trailing edge of what was called the silent generation. The stereotype—we were timid, gray flannel-suited—was more right than wrong. Conventional wisdom decreed that, insofar as students cared about politics at all (and few did), their future was tilting rightward. In 1960, Young Americans for Freedom (YAF), sponsored by William F. Buckley, started with more than one hundred delegates from forty-four colleges and universities, while SDS, relaunched at Port Huron, Michigan, in 1962, drew only fifty-nine from twelve campuses. In 1962, YAF could fill Madison Square Garden; SDS could never have managed such a turnout either logistically or numerically. The Left had the numbers only in civil rights—at least in the North. Most of the white South contented itself with white supremacy. Still, even there, tiny numbers triggered huge movements. The black students who launched the sit-in movement at a lunch counter in Greensboro, N.C., February 1, 1960, numbered four.

Small numbers promoted our philosophical mood, which in some nondoctrinal way was existentialist. We believed we defined ourselves by our actions, not our ideology, our *ism* or our culture. We did not consult polls to get with the zeitgeist. We knew there are no guarantees. We were proud not to have them—not even to need them. Our bravest organizers (I do not include myself in this company) plunged into darkness not because it was stylish or because they were proud possessors of a theory that assured them that they were destined to win but *because they decided to overcome fear*, period. During much of the decade, the end of the tunnel looked dark. The Deep South consisted of terror states. For years, the war in Vietnam was popular. Even as the movement grew, the corpses piled up and the war looked unstoppable. Toward the end of the sixties came the dope-fueled, wild-in-the-streets quest for the hippie synthesis, "Revolution for the hell of it," as Abbie Hoffman said—having your cake and wolfing it down, too. But poor manic-depressive Abbie mistook his state of mind for the state of the world—a common error in revolutionary times, even the faux ones. You *can't* have it all.

In other words, we weren't historical opportunists. True, we shared with our apolitical agemates a certain generational confidence (at times a larky smugness, an excess of bravado) that came from fifties-bred, post–World War II affluence and Kennedy's boost to the can-do spirit. The Pill was dandy too. But often enough we were stumbling around fearing the worst. I never felt that the movement was made up of sunshine kids out for a frolic or that we were bound to prevail. The Freedom Riders who took buses to southern towns where they knew they would be greeted by racist mobs, the civil rights workers in Mississippi who tried to register voters and collided with murderous Klansmen—you can't lump together these heroes with their vastly more numerous contemporaries whose most fervent ambition was to get on *American Bandstand*. We who (much less riskily) marched against nuclear weapons, against the Vietnam War and in a hundred other causes were not so sure we were destined for glory. Often enough, when the glow from the latest demonstration subsided, we were left with the nagging question, Now what?—an inch away from despair.

Our climate was soaked in atrocity. For more than a decade, every day the world *felt* dire. Let me make "the cold war" a little less abstract. Throughout the late fifties and early sixties, the U.S. and U.S.S.R. were setting off nuclear bombs routinely, to prove how prepared they were for Armageddon. My generation was dragooned into ridiculous bomb drills—"Take cover!" your teacher burst out in the middle of a lesson, and you crouched beneath your tiny desk, pretending that your crumpled posture would save you from vaporization and radiation death. If you'd been paying attention, the Cuban missile crisis of 1962 wasn't a bolt from the blue, it was a glaring reminder that nuclear war was plausible. Kennedy and Khrushchev came to their senses (with the help of Pope John XXIII) and the Bomb went into abeyance. In 1963, détente became respectable and nuclear tests went underground—with some help, let it be said, from the ban the bomb, stop the tests movement—but no sooner had the menace of future conflagration gone pale than Vietnam cropped up, an everyday conflagration in real time.

After the worst of the cold war, no cool peace. If you were sensitized to the lunacy of international relations, you could see worse coming. In Vietnam, a war with no clear beginning ratcheted up. By 1963, savage war by the U.S. against Communists was on. In 1965, the U.S. was bombing Vietnam, North and South, every day, the marines had landed, the napalm was dropping—and that was just the known part of the war. Living with the knowledge that our country perpetrates moral abominations is an everyday burden. The next time you yearn for the glamour years of the sixties, please also bear in mind the steady carnage in Vietnam, unbearable events that we had to learn to endure because we were powerless to stop them. Say all you want about the lark we were on: our one and only lives were stunted by sheer knowledge of the crimes and stupidities being committed in our names every day. Strangely, miraculously, we still had a picnic—an interrupted picnic—but it wasn't because the world was sweet or nourishing or because we were sunny American kids bound for glory. Over the days, weeks, months, years, a senseless war piled up corpses by the hundreds, thousands, tens of thousands, hundreds of thousands, and the arguments for it were so shoddy, the damage done so disproportionate to the force of the arguments mounted in its behalf, we despaired of reason. One SDS organizer used to say that we were organizing to prevent "the seventh war from now."

To return to the glumness you may feel in the face of the larger-than-life sixties, and the alibis that pop into the minds of inactivists: Both stem from fashion thinking, and all fashion thinking is suspect; it's not actual thinking but a reflex. Generational blocs do not march like unified phalanxes. In the true down-on-the-ground sixties, radicalism was not all of a piece. Sex–drugs–rock 'n' roll, the soft part, was not glued to political radicalism, the hard part. The movement was not a costume party. By 1968 and 1969, it's certainly true that millions of college students and others felt affiliated with the movement. Many more smoked marijuana and dropped acid, and millions more abandoned bras, grew hair long, enjoyed easy sex—or thought they ought to and, moreover,

feel less neurotic about it. (Just how much sexier in practice the sixties were than the fifties remains doubtful.)
Media amplified the notion that letting the id flow loose
was the temper of the time. Millions went to demonstrations, at least once in a while; but for most of the sixties,
the political side was not so fashionable. The core of the
movement was pretty small. At its peak, the Student
Nonviolent Coordinating Committee (SNCC) numbered perhaps 200 field organizers. There were a few
score Freedom Riders, and 1,000 volunteers for Mississippi Summer. When I was elected president of Students
for a Democratic Society in 1963, we had 1,100 members, 600 of whom had paid their dues, and (on paper)
nineteen chapters. The first national demonstration
against the war in Vietnam, in Washington, D.C., April
17, 1965, numbered 25,000—which felt huge.

Moreover, the war in Vietnam was popular in the
country at large. It started out popular and stayed popular for a couple of brutal years. In August 1964, after
President (and peace candidate) Lyndon B. Johnson
replied to a dubious naval incident in the Tonkin Gulf
off the coast of North Vietnam with reprisal air strikes,
Congress tendered him carte blanche authority (without
any time limits) "to take all necessary measures to repel
any armed attacks against the forces of the United States
and to prevent further aggression"—against all of *two*
dissents in the Senate and not a single dissent in the
House. Polled support for Johnson's policy zoomed
from 58 percent to 85 percent. In February 1965, similar
numbers supported the escalation of steady bombing
raids in North Vietnam. This sort of automatic lineup is

a national tradition: students of public opinion call it the rally-round-the-flag effect.

Such popular support would seem to bolster the rather heroic notion that the antiwar campuses resisted the martial tide. Another legend. Antiwar events and publicity to the contrary notwithstanding, the war in fact was consistently most popular with the college-educated population and least popular with those who never graduated high school, according to polls. As the war dragged on, the class base of the active antiwar movement deepened, but through 1967 or so, outside elite schools, opposing the war was not all the rage.

Administrators, police and mobs cracked down on antiwar activists without much dissent. In October 1965, when an activist at Tulsa University invited SDS to send an antiwar speaker, I volunteered, but the administration refused to permit me to speak—or even debate—on campus. When I went to Tulsa anyway, I had to speak in an off-campus coffeehouse. That wasn't abnormal. The same year, at Kent State University, thirty antiwar activists were met by a rock-throwing crowd five times larger. A few antiwar students at Michigan State were charged with trespassing, jailed and bound in chains, while 16,000 students signed prowar petitions. The *New York Daily News*, the country's largest circulation newspaper at the time, demanded that "Communist-incited beatniks, pacifists and damned idiots" be tried for treason. At Texas A&M, prowar students sent a sixty-foot telegraph of support to LBJ, while the following year, a few students handing out antiwar flyers were arrested by campus police, who drove them eighty miles away and told them not to come back.

Poll results are always tricky to assess, but for what they're worth: At the end of 1965, one in four Americans thought antiwar demonstrators "tools of the communists," and one-third thought they had "no right to demonstrate." Two years later, the latter number had risen to 40 percent, and in the spring of 1969 it was up to 52 percent. A staggering 82 percent of Americans believed that student demonstrators ought to be expelled from school.

So nothing was effortless about the antiwar movement; it wasn't, in that imprecise and evasive cliché, an expression of the times. The times were profoundly polarized. It wasn't that impersonal and irresistible cliché of textbooks and punditry, the times, that caused antiwar sentiment; closer to the truth is that the antiwar sentiment caused the times. Only as the number of troops—and American casualties—multiplied, and the antiwar movement kept pushing, did war support stall. Not until the fall of 1967, after years of growing war, did more Americans think the intervention a mistake than not. Not until March 31, 1968, when Lyndon Johnson announced he would not run for another term, did more Americans describe themselves as doves than hawks.

None of this is to say that minorities always prevail, or that it's always a good thing when they do. They have to make sense—which means make sense to the locals, at least some critical mass of them. You are not permitted to dissolve the people and elect a new one, as Bertolt Brecht mockingly advised the East German government during the workers' revolt of 1953. To influence events, activists must connect to the public—which means however cosmopolitan or internationalist you aspire to be, the public elects governments. Archimedes is supposed to have said that with a lever, he could move the world. Yet he also needed a fulcrum, a place to stand. Hallucinations will not do. Fantasies of an ideal realm will not do. That place to stand must always be solid, substantial, right here at hand.

Another sixties burden weighs on today's activists oppositely. This is the right-wing myth that the radicalism of the sixties indeed was all the rage but produced nothing but barbarism and moral decline. In this view, the antiwar movement is responsible for Communist hell in Southeast Asia; the culture of sexual liberation is responsible for AIDS and out-of-wedlock births; feminism produces latchkey children, crippled manhood and casual abortions; education reform produces political correctness, grade inflation, dumbing down and so on. (It's considered bad form to knock the civil rights movement openly, though Republican heroes such as Barry Goldwater and Ronald Reagan did so quite guiltlessly at the time.) From this point of view, activists of the Left are at best naïve, at worst destructive. This right-wing revelry about the barbaric sixties resonates in popular lore that greets all grand ideals with a shrug.

It is a hoary warning, a backbeat to Enlightenment hope from the French Revolution onward, this conviction that those who try to improve the world only make it worse, because reason run amok becomes a blueprint to tyranny. As Albert O. Hirschman wrote in *The Rhetoric of Reaction*, the argument about the infernal consequences of good intentions is a longtime implement of the political Right—which does not automatically make it inaccurate. Ironic knowingness deliciously suits the in-activist too. Yet however self-serving, the argument deserves to be taken seriously—which means concretely. The right view of the sixties is neither thumbs up nor thumbs down. We have more fingers than that.

Cheerleaders for left-wing upheaval had better face this uncomfortable fact: The argument about perverse consequences sometimes holds more than a grain of truth. On Vietnam, it's weakest. The war was a slaughter-house that only staved off an inevitable defeat for liberty, democracy and other Western values. If anything, the nonstop American war bolstered the hard-line views of the hardest of hard-liners within the Communist Party. But communism, wrapped in Ho Chi Minh's national-ism, the prime carrier of the rebellion against French colonialism, was bound to prevail one way or the other. Had it prevailed in 1954 or 1963, two or three million more Vietnamese would have remained alive and there's no reason to believe the regime would have been more repressive than it turned out—arguably it would have been less so. Since the American war in addition had the perverse consequence of strengthening Cambodia's Khmer Rouge, which in its brief reign proved unspeak-ably more murderous than Vietnamese communism, the genocidally perverse consequences of pursuing the war far outweigh any good results.

What about the purportedly barbaric consequences of sixties movements, the corrosion of culture induced by the liberationist impulse? The standard conservative trope is that an effusion of id and disrespect set America, in the title of a book by Judge Robert Bork, slouching toward Gomorrah. As with all modern nostalgias, the problem is to identify the Golden Age that preceded to-day's fool's gold or tinsel. Sometimes it's premodern, sometimes Victorian, sometimes as recent as the fifties. In Bork's version, the sixties, a carnival of freedom, smashed up the fifties, a repository of order, resulting in crime, drugs, abortion, divorce, teenage pregnancy, out-of-wedlock birth, a welfare binge and a general disrespect for authority. Drinking deep of the draught of despair, political scientist Harvey C. Mansfield typically maintains that the late sixties were "a comprehensive disaster" that did "measureless harm."

Fundamentalisms of different stripes share a particular dismay at women's freedom. Feminism, writes political scientist Jeremy Rabkin, became "a showcase for the least attractive impulses in the radicalism of the sixties," damaging families, depriving children, undermining the values of working-class women in behalf of the upper tiers. Feminism was (and despite backlash, remains) an immensity—an extension of principles of equality and dignity to more than half the human race. The emancipation of women, despised by fundamentalist totalitarians under various religious sponsorship, is one of those historical ideas whose time had come virtually everyplace where fundamentalist patriarchs did not hold sway—indeed, it is a long-running tendency in the West and increasingly (though against determined opposition à la Taliban) elsewhere. True enough, the women's convulsion that sprang from the late sixties generated some rigidified thinking and social harm. Like all movements contemptuous of stability and intoxicated by their sense of momentum—including conservative movements—feminist zealots sometimes failed to reckon on the damage they did, were sometimes indifferent to children, sometimes thought badly. Yet a more rigorous exploration of the immense changes in women's roles and family life shows that they swept with equivalent force across societies everywhere, and that despite some material downsides—especially for impoverished women abandoned to fend for themselves—the advances in dignity are not willingly retracted by the majority whom conservatives think are either unwitting victims or negligent mothers. The drive to protect women against male violence and sexual exploitation spreads because most women welcome it. Note that divorce and unmarried cohabitation did soar in societies where feminism thrived (the U.S. and Scandinavia, for example) but also in societies where the feminist movement was weak (France and Italy, for example).

As for the direct material consequences of sixties liberationism, a little argumentative care will get us a long way. To blame the spread of the AIDS epidemic on sixties gay liberation is vicious victim thumping: It falsely—indeed, maliciously—assumes that in the seventies and early eighties gays knew about the HIV virus. (This is like blaming the World Trade Center's architect for the massacre of September 11.) Once the link between the virus and unprotected sex became known, however, it's legitimate to fault the johnny-come-lately devil-may-care practitioners of unprotected sex—both gay and straight. As for the drug epidemics of postsixties decades, surely sixties drug tolerance was a *necessary* condition of the drug boom, for given the demand, markets flourished, as free-marketeers will understand. But sixties tolerance, giddy as it was, hardly ever extended to the ruinous drugs—heroin, cocaine, speed and such. Blame sixties naïveté for failing to grasp the dangers of even softer drugs in excess, but make sure it shares the blame with the self-discrediting prohibitionist, prosecutorial zeal whose answer is lock 'em up, and with the indiscriminate consumerism that stuffs our lives with gadgets and analgesics as pseudo-solutions to every problem. The sixties and postsixties critique of the drug war—critique of its efficacy—remains decidedly apropos.

Liberal society needs conservatives. As sociologist Philip Slater has argued, all societies embody contrary principles. A good measure of equipoise is healthy. Someone has to resist unrestrained social change whenever it moves "too far" in any single direction—and the debate as to where too far starts is always useful. Brakes are the health in the conserving impulse. But when conservatives blame domestic enemies for epochal extensions of democratic and individual rights, they are refusing to face the complexity and strangeness of culture. When they savage liberationist movements while approving of unbridled markets whose business is to stir up consumer desire and cut individuals loose from the institutions that tether them, they lend their imprimatur to an economic system that, for all its achievements, is surely the most revolutionary, tradition-undermining, desire-unleashing force in the history of the world. They want to keep selfishness where it belongs—in the executive suites and the mall. Why this is the voice of morality escapes me.

Still, let us be generous, turn down the volume of the rhetorical blasts against Gomorrah, and acknowledge that the road of excess (to paraphrase William Blake) may lead the excessive themselves to the palace of wisdom but may also land fellow travelers in the ditch of delusion. The same question worth asking about the sixties is worth asking about history as a whole: What follows from the perverse consequences argument? Unpleasant it might be to say so, but every just course of action in history entails damage. Goodness does not win pretty—regardless of the intentions of the good. The benefits of industrial capitalism, including its relative comforts, imposed centuries of ordeals along the way: the uprooting of the peasantry, work discipline cruelties, the enslavement of Africans to produce a standard of living high enough to reward a substantial part of the industrializing population. For the inheritors, these ordeals paid off, in some sense, but often not for those who paid the costs. To end slavery in the United States, more than 600,000 soldiers died, not counting civilians—had to die, it is fair to say, in a war of unparalleled brutality; but just what was the alternative? The victory against Nazi Germany ushered in Soviet totalitarian rule over Eastern and Central Europe lasting almost half a century. Decolonization after the British and French empires ushered in many tyrannies. The end of apartheid in South Africa resulted in an explosion in crime. So did the collapse of communism. Further examples come easily to mind. Rewards are never unbridled. So be it.

But the historian's wisdom is the activist's dilemma. A tragic view of history does not fit so well on a sloganeer's placard. "Half an evil is better than the whole hog" would seem to lack something in inspirational value. "Inch ahead" promises few recruits. "CAUTION: You could make everything worse" invites cowardice. How much discouragement can you take on before it paralyzes you? The answer is, more than you think. Over the long haul, you will probably do more good if you accept that history is a Möbius strip—that the topside turns into the underside, that the romance of the revolution to end all revolutions is as dangerous as it is delusional—than if you pretend that the sun is always rising in America. The price of intellectual honesty is high, but not as high as blindness. (The difference is that the intellectually dishonest, like Lenin, usually force other people to pay the price for their own tunnel vision.)

You've already discovered that optimism is balm. Certitude, not agnosticism, makes the blood race—not least in America, which cherishes a victory culture (in Tom Engelhardt's phrase). But be careful: If you're giddy with expectations, like the revolutionists of the late sixties, your giddiness will work on you like a drug—until, if you're lucky, you crash, and if you're unlucky, something worse happens. This was the way of the Communists and their fellow travelers, who were always looking to explain (away) any criticisms of the Soviet Union as fabrications of the bourgeois press, malevolent distractions from the true world-historical mission of marching onward toward socialism. The equivalent rapture was the fate of too many hard-core activists of my generation, who mistook their dizzy desires for real revolutionary prospects and imagined that one surrogate working class or the other was at hand, the brawn that would put their brains to good use. Often they looked outward for ideals, hallucinating that popular equality had come to

China, Cuba, North Vietnam, even North Korea and the Khmer Rouge's Cambodia, and that reports of atrocities must be press exaggerations or, perhaps, "understandable" reactions. The apologist's rule of thumb is that freedom is highly selective: Left-wing governments do good because they *are* good, and if they are bad at all, that can only be because America forced them.

The dream of the apocalypse, when once and for all the last become first and the righteous purge themselves of impurities, is a temptation perennially renewed. Even in today's chastened circumstances you will find the disingenuous, the cynical and the naïve who look on the bright side of tyrants, domestic or foreign, as long as they are dark-skinned. These groups are tiny but disciplined, always ready, never surprised. In a crisis such as that which followed September 11, they are quick to thaw out, to meet, pass out leaflets, organize demonstrations and rallies, for they can readily define every new situation as a repeat of an old situation, so no fresh thinking is required.

Saviors are always tempted by angels. Their passion for heroes disguises a mission of self-rescue. The passion to march to a flourish of trumpets wherever they lead helps them overlook obstacles that can't be wished away. So, for one thing, they overestimate their potential numbers. (Thus, for example, black radicals fail to take seriously that African Americans number about 12 percent of the population.) For another thing, saviors are quick to apologize for (a.k.a. "understand") crimes that, if carried out by enemies, they would condemn. There can be no enemies to their Left. (After the 1978 murder-suicide of the People's Temple in Guyana, one well-known Bay Area leftist insisted to me that the CIA had driven the Rev. Jim Jones crazy in order to discredit socialism.) In the grip of the need to believe that they are on the right side of history, they look to the postcolonial tyrant, the *líder máximo*. They find reasons to believe that terrorist mass murderers are vengeful though possibly excessive and misguided anti-imperialist angels dispatched on behalf of the wretched of the earth, though "of course" their depredations, while deplorable, are not nearly as significant as the depredations of American Empire. If you believe such things, you are riding for a fall—not only a moral fall but a practical one, for you cannot possibly win more than a smidgen of popular support for positions that defy common sense.

Fortunately, your generation seems less giddy than mine, less gullible—so far. Please go on leaving the victory marches and the catch tunes to the tinny bands. The long-distance runner listens to the blues.

So take the sixties not as a burden but a prologue. Neither a worshiper nor a cynic be. The world didn't begin the day you were born and it won't end the day you die. You did not choose the world, but you must choose how to live in it, and you can't live in it without recognizing it for what it is, and you can't do *that* without knowing history. Ignorance of the past may be an excuse for people with lesser ambitions than changing the world, but it's no excuse for you. Paying attention to history (not just the sixties, by the way—not by a long shot) will help you improve on your predecessors. They—we—made mistakes, which is one (though only one) reason why the world remains to be changed—and while the situation you confront is always different from what your predecessors confronted, the best way to free yourself from their shadow is to walk a while in their shoes.

3

■ On Idealism and Right Action,
or Nonviolence Unexhausted

Dear ——,

It's often said, sometimes warmly, sometimes scorn-
fully, that the sixties were awash in idealism. (By implication, your generation falls short.) Awash, yes. Ideals ran
rampant, all sorts of ideals: about political and social
arrangements, living arrangements, offbeat religions and
cultural styles. Moral earnestness was in flower. In 1968,
42 percent of college students thought that the main
goal of college was intangible, including "the opportunity to change things"; the rest said that their goals were
practical: to make more money, improve their careers
and social positions. Authority came unstuck, and freedom—at least the aspiration to freedom—felt almost
normal. Feeling marooned in a cynical era, you look
back longingly. Ideals do not embarrass you, and you
wish you had more company.

Some sociologists will tell you that high-flying ideals
of human potential were by-products of prosperity.

(When this sentence is repeated in a cynical tone, it sounds like this: If there's a material base for ideals, ideals are derivative, in which case they've been put in their place, in which case they're not all they're cracked up to be; idealists don't deserve quite so much credit, and maybe we're better off without them in the first place.) Most college students didn't have to work. You could afford to drop out for a year or two because you knew— even unconsciously—that should you decide to drop back in, the world would be waiting to reward you in the manner that you and your parents expected. Real estate values were no object: You could rent a decent apartment for $100 a month almost anywhere. Why *not* frolic a bit, bum around, do civil rights or draft resistance, write for an underground paper or live in a commune?

Whether or not the material base was a necessary condition for idealism, ideals are surely more modest and tentative now. At least this is the conventional wisdom. Surely much more energy goes into small-scale service than big social change efforts today. So two images, two spirits, two moments in history seem to square off against each other. Today, the realistic spirit of service: planting gardens, feeding and sheltering the homeless, tutoring students. The emotion: compassion. The slogan: Make a difference. Teach for America. In the sixties: radicalism, which usually (not always) entailed militant tactics such as organizing sit-ins and picket lines, and otherwise confronting authority. The emotion: anger. The slogan: We want the world and we want it now. The implication of this comparison is usually: We're grown up now. No more *kumbaya*. Get real. Be pragmatic, demand results.

This black-and-white diagram is simplistic and seriously distorted. It's predicated on a melodramatic tale about those far gone and glorious sixties when moral seriousness entailed spontaneous action and street fighters stalked the land—Lights! Camera! Cops! Dissolve to Viet Cong flags flapping in the breeze to the soundtrack of "Street Fighting Man"! During most of the sixties, idealism was nowhere near universal. Movement earnestness and longing were conspicuous by contrast with the more extensive vogue of hard practicality. At Kennedy-era Harvard, for example, we not-very-embarrassed idealists were greatly outnumbered by the unembarrassable realists under the tutelage of Henry Kissinger, think-tankers in training who, when they didn't despise us for our softness, condescended to us that we had no idea how the world worked. John F. Kennedy himself was an interesting mélange of realist and idealist, the former predominating, the latter dancing attendance with the Peace Corps. But this administration's dominant tone was set by McGeorge Bundy, national security advisor, former Harvard dean and one of the brightest lights of his best and brightest entourage. Hearing several of us demonstration leaders defend our ideals (in what we thought a rather hard-headed way) in a West Wing meeting during an anti-nuclear rally in Washington in 1962, Bundy said—with the knowing smile that throughout his entire career seemed frozen on his preternaturally smooth face—"Politics is the art of the possible." After Kennedy was murdered, Bundy did his ample part to imagine that (or act as if) an impossible victory in Vietnam was indeed possible, thus saddling realism with a reputation for unreality and sending Democratic politics into an abyss.

Outside the marginal Left, in realistic America, unblinking ideals were a subterranean stream of sensibility—a counterfashion. Borrowed from Quaker and other dissenting Christian traditions, the movement's earnest, straightforward, unambiguous "We Shall Overcome," "We Shall Not Be Moved" and "Study War No More" fell in with a major stream of popular culture—folk music, Simon and Garfunkel, early Beatles, Motown. Defying the cant of sincerity, the put-on had a certain vogue among sophisticates, as did the political satire of Lenny Bruce and Mort Sahl, but there was no *Saturday Night Live* to turn the ironic screw in suburban living rooms. During the Vietnam War, slogans ran toward unconditional statements of principle: "Make Love, Not War"; "War Is Not Healthy for Children and Other Living Things." Realists never ceased despising utopian ideals as sentimental evasions, but social critics such as C. Wright Mills, Erich Fromm and Paul Goodman kept thundering against government lies, corporate irresponsibility and everyday corruption.

Idealism became a central cultural style, integral to the sixties' shining glory (and tragic hubris too). Yet stand-alone idealism was not the deep truth about activism or its paramount achievement. Serious activists recognized that idealism actually shielded the status quo by appearing so exotic that it renounced any hope of serious influence, leaving center stage to the tough guys of realism. Idealism—a quality of feeling—needed to be completed by action. The sixties' genius lay in applying ideals to activity. The movement understood that what makes the world move is not wanting the right ideals, not even wanting them intensely, but intelligently turning ends into means—or in the terms of Eastern religion, converting the want into the right action (Buddhism) or the right way (Taoism). A homier version of the principle is, When cutting up a chicken, don't cut wildly—cut at the joints.

The principle behind the passion had to be righteous, but righteous intention could not be trusted to express itself spontaneously. Right action requires thought: a realistic appraisal of the world of institutions and powers, of actual and potential adversaries and allies. To think or feel the right thing wasn't enough; the right thought had to catch the popular imagination. The right passion had to engage a wider public, had to make itself unignorable. The small engine of ideals had to ignite the larger engine of popular movement. When we called ourselves the movement, we signaled this whole process, for we were not only on the move ourselves, we imagined ourselves—this was our home-grown version of realism—moving the whole society, energy converting to mass. The movement imagination was grounded—not airy, not arbitrary, not fantastical. The question was not only, What do you want? but, How do you propose to get it?

The definitive sixties action was the sit-in, a tactic that is commonly misunderstood. On the surface, the sit-in protests a bad situation by nonviolently breaking the law. You get arrested—if it comes to that—but you take the moral high ground. You help yourself with theatrics, dressing up, for example, as did the four students who sat down at a white-only lunch counter in Greensboro, N.C., on February 1, 1960, asking to be served and deciding not to take no for an answer, even as they were assaulted by white racists and eventually dragged away and arrested. Your arrest mobilizes the public in your behalf, and eventually the law changes. The genius of the sit-in, however, ran deeper than the civil rights slogan "Put your body on the line," later enlarged upon in Mario Savio's famous Free Speech Movement metaphor of the machine, "You've got to put your bodies upon the gears and upon the wheels, upon the levers, upon all the apparatus, and you've got to make it stop," at a crucial moment in Berkeley's 1964 Free Speech Movement. The sit-in was a deep tactic inseparable from strategy, a means that prefigured the end. The sit-in was not an outsider's demand, a request delivered to politicians in hope that they would do the right thing. Not a protest or a negative act of disobedience, it was an affirmation, a prefiguration, an act of fertility—a creative act designed to engender a new situation.

The sit-in has a root in the anarchist and socialist traditions. In principle, it resembles a union, which is more than a means to better wages and working conditions. Union solidarity is meant to be a cornerstone principle of a more egalitarian society. It's meant to plant the seeds of "a new society in the shell of the old." (The more chillingly militant version was, "A new world in the ashes of the old.") At least in the radical interpretation, the labor sit-ins of the thirties—the worker occupations at auto and steel plants—were declarations that the workers could run factories without parasitical management. In the same spirit, the civil rights sit-in proclaimed that racial segregation is wrong, unconscionable—but also, finally, it is a *collaboration*, out of fear. It rests on popular willingness to go along, with whites and blacks each playing their duly assigned roles. We who sit in withdraw our willingness. *We don't deplore segregation, we abolish it.* When we cross the color line and sit down in a white-only bus seat or at a lunch counter, we inaugurate a new way of life. When the authorities act to suppress this little utopia that we've launched, they convict themselves in the court of public opinion. We suffer, but—be patient— *they fail.*

The movement was a school for spontaneity. Activists educated activists. May I briefly retell one tale? When, in the fall of 1964, the authoritarian University of California administration banned off-campus political activities at Berkeley (can you imagine?), one activist— Jack Weinberg, a veteran of Mississippi travails—gamely went about his business recruiting for civil rights in the main campus plaza. When a police car drove onto the campus to cart him away, October 1, 1964, other activists surrounded the car, sat down and refused to move. Speakers hoisted themselves onto the roof to give speeches. (They were so polite, they took off their shoes first.) Thousands collected there that day, that night, then the next day. The police were isolated—literally. Students were teachers. They stayed there for thirty-two hours while a deal was worked out. No one who was there forgets the communal spirit, the mutual trust, straight out of Gandhi. Right action but also playfulness. This was how the Free Speech Movement began— freely, with speech, and movingly.

Sit-ins spawned other, similar tactics—teach-ins, for example. A teach-in, as devised by antiwar faculty at the University of Michigan in March 1965, was not meant to be synonymous with a rally. Contrary to the current loose usage, a teach-in was an intensely educational moment—the original antiwar teach-in in Ann Arbor went on all night—bringing academic expertise to bear on life-and-death questions about Vietnam and the cold war that, however urgent, had been neglected in the university curriculum. At a moment of urgency, it produced, at what Maria Montessori would call "a teachable moment," an intense if transitory (partly *because* transitory) school within a fossilized school, a model of intellectual seriousness that was at the same time convivial. Legally speaking, teach-ins were not civil disobedience, but their spirit was the same: beyond protest, to create, in the heart of the present, traces of a superior way of life.

Thanks to informal networks of antiwar professors, the teach-ins spread with amazing speed. The few American intellectuals who knew Vietnam suddenly found a hearing. For the sake of debate, sometimes organizers invited State Department officials to state their own case; sometimes professor-surrogates substituted for them. For the movement, this was a shrewd move as well as a principled one. State Department cant proved feeble against antiwar expertise, and quickly the State Department stopped playing along. Despite the government's cold war success in buying fine brains—the fruit of a generation's worth of subsidies—the Vietnam fantasists in Washington were maladroit. Their arguments flopped. The more they talked, the more they lost support. The teach-ins, in other words, tapped the movement's strength on its own ground—its knowledge. They fit their setting—the academy. They spoke to their constituents—students and teachers. They did not shriek or mourn—they organized.

To succeed, a campaign of civil disobedience has to be farsighted, strategic. It does not hope to reinvent the world at will. It does not simply express itself. It must make arguments and defeat contrary arguments. It must take place within history, not beat on its doors from outside. It must seize opportunities (and in this sense can properly be called opportunistic). It must call on popular (even if latent) convictions and sentiments. Timing matters greatly. From Gandhi onward, successful civil disobedience campaigns have mobilized preponderant numbers in the right way to ignite the right reaction. Just so, Gandhi and seventy-eight campaigners started by protesting the British salt tax on a march to the sea in 1930. The salt march attracted thousands and went on from there. After two decades of nonviolent struggle, his movement prevailed. India drove out the British because the British were vastly outnumbered *and* had neither an insuperable stake in subduing India nor a conscienceless commitment to ruthless suppression. In this spirit, the southern civil rights movement brandished the Declaration of Independence, the Emancipation Proclamation, and the post–Civil War amendments to the Constitution—all these great American achievements in the Enlightenment tradition—against white supremacist usurpations. In the theater of politics, the southern claim that "states rights" trumped "Washington policies" appeared as racist and mean-spirited as it is. Symbolized by police dogs, cattle prods and water hose barrages against children, segregationist resistance crumbled. In the unlikely person of Lyndon B. Johnson, Enlightenment principle triumphed.

Obviously, civil disobedience is no panacea. The timing must be right, the tactic, apt. Originality counts. One size does not fit all. The first Freedom Rides were undertaken by the Congress of Racial Equality in 1947, but at least partly because no television news existed to push their story to prominence, they went nowhere. A group of interracial bus passengers, trying to force the federal government to uphold a Supreme Court ruling that segregated seating of interstate passengers was unconstitutional, were arrested in North Carolina without much to-do and sent to a chain gang for six months. No movement ignited. In South Africa, civil disobedience went nowhere: The apartheid regime hadn't the scruples to relinquish its power against a nonviolent campaign; the whites had the guns and were willing to use them. Even when civil disobedience succeeds, it does not automatically usher in a good society. Gandhi's great campaign ended in religious partition, the terrible Hindu-Muslim riots in which some two million people were slaughtered—and the assassination of Gandhi himself. More than half a century later, India and Pakistan are nuclear powers, their armies of hundreds of millions glaring at each other—if, by the time you read this, they have not indeed leaped off the brink. So again (how many times!), humanity resists any effort at streamlining. Nothing here but dilemmas.

Let's not exaggerate either the powers of nonviolence in America. In the sixties, there were limits not only to the efficacy of civil disobedience but to its prevalence. Even in the Deep South, where the movement created brilliant nonviolent theater, civil rights leadership was more committed to nonviolent principle than followers.

Many practiced it only tactically—they knew they were badly outgunned. Some had no time for Christian cheek turning. The American South was gun country to start with. In the murderous Deep South, under siege by racist terrorists, bands of local blacks such as Louisiana's Deacons for Defense and Justice armed themselves against the Ku Klux Klan, serving as bodyguards and escorts for grateful civil rights workers. When fired on by racist vigilantes, they fired back. This was a practical, directly defensive use of violence—not bombastic, not media driven. Still, violent self-defense was rare. Nonviolence maintained the initiative. Look at practical results and the conclusion is irresistible that the civil rights movement won its great victories for voting and other political rights and against segregation under the sway of nonviolence—or nonviolence with an asterisk. As Randall Kennedy has argued, these victories dwarfed the accomplishments of the movement's postnonviolent phase.

Maybe what's old-fashioned is not civil disobedience but violent action and violent rhetoric—stale nineteenth-century gestures. Nonviolence aimed at specific private and public targets, meanwhile, is far from exhausted—witness the campaigns to get AIDS drugs developed and released (I'll write more about that in my next letter). Companies that run sweatshops, chop down rain forests, help melt the icecaps and still hope to win public esteem are vulnerable, since plutocracy is more flagrant and conspicuous nowadays, and the tide that raised CEOs to stupendous heights left most stockholders beached. Inventive tactics impress the general public, while corporate P.R. doesn't look so compelling anymore.

But you're a realist—you ask with a quick grin whether this isn't what I want you to be—and you have an argument for the practicality of at _ st some violent tactics. You insist that violence worked—or a combination of violence and the threat of more—not by coming out onstage but by lurking conspicuously in the wings. You note that in the latter sixties nonviolence was wearing thin and succumbing to rage. You point to all the urban riots, local uprisings, really, a whole rippling popular movement of them in the sixties. You note that even while Martin Luther King was alive, the movement initiative was passing to avenging angels such as Malcolm X—and later Stokely Carmichael, Rap Brown, the Black Panthers and various violent groupuscules that spun off in their wake. You note that King's assassination silenced the angel of nonviolence, leaving the rhetorical initiative to the avatars of Black Power and Revolution who attracted the media spotlight—and that partly but not entirely for this reason, they recruited the most fervent of militants, half-plausibly arguing that nonviolent methods were ill-suited to the obstacles faced by black Americans after the civil rights and voting reforms of the mid sixties.

I'll acknowledge that you're right, up to a point, about one thing: The threats brought some results. Resources flowed into the impoverished black sector partly because the white establishment quivered at the thought of "the fire next time." But—and this is crucial—if you want to assign any credit to these blasts of threat, you have to acknowledge the downside too. Black communities were devastated—some, more than thirty years later, still not rebuilt. Doesn't such damage outweigh the momentary exultation of looters, arsonists and snipers? Not only that, but the riots, threats and violent rhetoric panicked much of the white electorate, stampeding them into the Republican Party, which proved adept at managing wedge issues and where many of them have lodged ever since. The Democratic Party that had set the national agenda between 1932 and 1968 would shudder anyway, as civil rights broke off the southern Dixiecrats, who, when push came to shove, preferred the pleasures of white supremacy to the economic principles of the New Deal. But panic worsened the white recoil, inflamed northern and western whites, boosted the Reaganite movement, and deepened the Left's discredit.

On the white Left, virtuoso nonviolence continued to crop up—most successfully in the draft resistance and GI movements—but the uglier the war became, the larger grew a movement core of experienced activists who dismissed what seemed to them a retro, wimpy tradition. They indulged the revolutionary fantasy that the counterwar ("two, three, many Vietnams," in a Cuban slogan) was spreading and winning. Capitalizing on this mood, in 1969, the Weathermen faction—speaking a Maoist-Guevaraist mishmash, tough-talking, sexing drugging and rock 'n' rolling—dismantled Students for a Democratic Society, the student movement's largest association. Soon they went underground, building bombs. They were not the only ones. Local networks resorted to arson at ROTC and military research buildings, explosions at electrical towers and the like—almost entirely against property, though a graduate student was killed when an antiwar squadron blew up the Army Math Research Center in Madison, Wisconsin, in August 1970. Violent activists won few friends and influenced a host of people—partisans and enemies of the movement, indifferents as well—uniting them in a shared abhorrence, tarring the rest of the movement. The nonviolent side of the movement was growing too, if we measure it by the numbers who turned out for peaceful demonstrations. Nonviolent protests grew, became more inventive, such as the 1969 Moratorium that across the country, from large cities to small towns, offered a range of tactics under the general heading, No business as usual. But the nonviolent majority lost sharpness. If for no other reason than that the media gravitate to bloodshed, nonviolence surrendered the spotlight. The stampede for order was on. The result was the momentous paradox of the late sixties: *even as the war became steadily less popular, so did the antiwar movement.* There may be countries (France?) where militant uprisings bring out the population's own native antiauthoritarianism, but America is not one of them.

Reasoning from history is always incomplete, if for no other reason than that we didn't follow the path we didn't follow. We'll always be in doubt about what would have happened if something that didn't happen *had* happened. Ask what-if questions, counterfactual questions, and history stands mute. But I will ask and answer one anyway: Was nonviolence doomed? Had Martin Luther King survived 1968, he would have plunged—he had already plunged—into a long overshadowing. He had lost many of the ghetto youth. Media would have dismissed him as yesterday's news. Yet when his violent rivals had flamed out, in prison, dead or hopelessly exiled, King likely would have remained standing. He had the discipline to outlast them. He had the religious and philosophical foundation—what Gandhi called *satyagraha*, soul force. He might have been able to make nonviolence over, make it fresh.

The spirit and stock of nonviolent tactics always needs replenishment. Like all forms of human action, nonviolence over time tends to degenerate into formula. The mechanical act is lifeless, the human act ceases to develop—then the whole project withers, because authorities learn how to react to what they've seen before. Nonetheless, we've witnessed periodic renewals of this tradition since the sixties: in the seventies, putting the lid on nuclear power; in the eighties, divesting from South Africa; in the late nineties and continuing, the upsurges grouped together (misleadingly, I'll argue later) as *antiglobalization*. We've seen roughly one wave per decade, as a student cohort shakes off the weight of the past and creates new occasions for releasing the power latent in nonviolent action. Despite these vivid episodes, the reputation of nonviolent action has dulled. During the annual celebration of King's birthday, January 21, amid the news blurbs and sound bites that pass for memorials, nonviolence does not feature. In everyday parlance, the term *nonviolent* is used mainly as an adjective for criminal acts—burglary, say, as opposed to assault. Civil disobedience, if acknowledged as a brilliant invention, is consigned to the black-and-white documentary footage of a bygone century.

It remains a deplorable given—deplorable and a given—that media vampires thirst for blood, so the apostles of violence who hover around the edges of nonviolent movements looking for ways to hijack the spotlight will always have a certain advantage. Whether they're kicking out Starbuck's windows in Seattle or trashing a McDonald's, riotous freeloaders stand a good chance of producing a photogenic spectacle and stealing center stage. A hundred people can start a riot even if ten thousand are wholly nonviolent. That hundred will exploit your ten thousand. The media are always ready to submit to the hijacking. ("If it bleeds, it leads.") You cannot expect anything different from organizations that run the news, who see the world as crime, clash and spectacle. Their prime business is attention getting, period. Your criticism won't change them. They will not promote the actions that you want them to promote just because you wish it. Their creativity is meager. So you'll be held accountable for the impression left by the whole ensemble that comes to be considered "the event"—the action, the official response, the images broadcast. Factually, you share responsibility with the other players. Practically, you'll be left holding the bag.

Two things follow. First, be alert to the novelty of your historical situation. When you search for right action, be original. You can't afford to overlook the media's thirst for novelty, but you shouldn't pander to it, either. They will use you for their purposes, which are largely sensational; you must strive to use them for your purposes, defeat their clichés, convey your deepest and most intelligent ideals. Be an entrepreneur in the original sense: Undertake something. Overcome the inertia of repetition. Put something on the face of the earth that wasn't there before. *Make it new*, as Ezra Pound wrote about poetry.

Second, if you don't like the freeloaders who hijack your events as backdrops for their spectacular riots, don't let sentimentality stand in your way. Make it clear—to them and to the public—that you don't welcome intruders who violate your principles. They are not part of your movement. They are parasites. They have contempt for you: They impose themselves to eviscerate your efforts. Their main interest in you is to recruit from you, to deplete you. There's a reason why these so-called anarchists, or the "black bloc," are often in cahoots with the police—in Genoa 2001, as in Chicago 1968. They are not your allies—they abuse your trust. They are disloyal to you. Don't let your sense of loyalty censor you in return.

4

On Anger, Rage and Guilt, or Temptations of Thinking with Your Blood

Dear ———,

But you object that I'm in squelch mode, obsessed with the damage wrought by violent action. You think I sound as though we have all the time in the world—when people are dying of preventable starvation, when icecaps are melting and species are going extinct and dire war is a button away. You say that I'm not taking your feelings seriously, I'm not honoring your rich, righteous fury (or glee), I'm a stranger to your passion.

Actually, I suspect you want to go further but you're too polite to say so. If I'm not mistaken, a little voice in your head is whispering hex words: white, male, established, old, Enlightenment. . . . I seem, disconcertingly, to share the establishment's annoyance with street anger or sheer disruptive frolics. I'm anxious Dad in the role of control freak. What you really think is that I'm passionless because I'm tired, that's all there is to it—or worse,

I've drifted dangerously close to the other side. When my friends and I were in your position and *our* elders lectured us on the virtues of moderation, we didn't listen to them. We thought they were tired, stuck, timid and reconciled. So why should you listen to me now?

Fair enough. But don't believe for a minute that if I care about reason it's because I'm dispassionate. My sense of urgency is as acute as ever. Like you, I believe— I want to believe—that my indignation begins in a spirit of tenderness. Where the indignation is missing, the tenderness is probably withered too. I know how it feels when your nerve endings go out to the Salvadoran coffee picker, the Bangladeshi textile worker, the battered wife, the displaced peasant, the unemployed steelworker, the child at the wrong end of the cruise missile, so that acting in their behalf feels like breathing. We both love the earth, want to keep it from being harmed, because it is not only the earth but your and my earth, and our children's. We both want to improve the prospects for life and dignity not only because it's right but because we have—and feel—a personal stake. We want to cut through the obfuscation and callousness. We feel tied up in knots. We get out our swords . . .

What I am trying to say is that the important thing is not what we feel but what we *do* with what we feel. The righteousness of our emotions is neither an argument nor a tactic. When my crowd was smart (which wasn't always), we were pretty clear about where our indignation belonged and where to channel it. At our best, we turned it on suitable targets and we aimed to win. Our anger was most productive when (1) we had good arguments, (2) we stayed nonviolent, (3) we won a hearing from serious-minded insiders, and (4) we mobilized outside forces. Then we could afford to offend a lot of well-meaning bystanders and still get results by making intelligent nuisances of ourselves.

The same principles applied in the eighties and nineties. A stunning example is the work of the playwright-activist Larry Kramer and the groups he helped organize (Gay Men's Health Crisis and ACT-UP), which succeeded in changing the rules for developing and distributing new HIV-AIDS drugs by disrupting public meetings, clamoring against pharmaceutical companies and government agencies, making pests of themselves, gaining the respect of their antagonists. Dr. Anthony S. Fauci, director of the National Institutes of Health's program on infectious disease, has said about the famously, theatrically angry Kramer: "There is no question in my mind that Larry helped changed medicine in this country. And he helped change it for the better. When all the screaming and the histrionics are forgotten, that will remain." Fauci, for twenty years Washington's leading voice in AIDS research, was, as reporter Michael Specter writes, "for many years . . . one of Kramer's most vilified targets." Note also that a target less wise than Fauci would not have coped with the insurgent attacks so constructively. (I'll have more to say on this in letter 6.)

To act on your feelings feels like the most natural thing in the world—compassion, love, indignation, longing for justice, anger; a noble sequence of feelings. But I know from experience that something happens to anger when it gets down inside you and stagnates. It congeals into rage, useless rage, more diffuse and less manageable than anger. I don't mean to say that the difference is always so easy to discern, but roughly, anger has an address, rage is broadcast. Anger wants change while rage demands, above all, punishment.

Rage is so wild and implacable because it erupts from something inward and obscure—often (not always) some vast, unfathomable guilt. For a liberal, sensitivity to the suffering of others implies guilt. What I am about to write may not apply to you, but my hunch is that it applies to people you know: You feel that as long as you do not act you permit a wrong, and so you become one of its coauthors. Men and women of the Right seem to enjoy their rage more guiltlessly. Complicity is not their outstanding emotion. They're at ease having enemies— in fact, they're ill at ease without them. The Left's rage, by contrast, is more likely an outer manifestation of guilt. Guilt is the inner manifestation, rage is the outer; they're coupled and explosive. Rage tries to choke off the sense of complicity, but always fails. The cycle renews.

When I first investigated the world, I found so much injustice, I felt on intimate terms with rage. I learned to cherish it as a sign of life, an overcoming of numbness, a blast at accommodation. Especially in the later sixties, I never felt more alive than when I was fired up. Fury was the source of transformative energy. It got harder to tell whether fury began with morality or vice versa. The corruptions of power, the cruelties and brutalities, the unfairness that leaves so many miserable when others prosper by the accident of birth—all this required purging, an absolute turning over, actual revolution. I discovered that, if rage made my blood run, militancy kept it running—if not the militancy of the streets, at least the militancy of theory and the armchair. No wonder that I intimately recognized the sentiment expressed by one militant in the late sixties: "I want to turn myself into a brick and hurl myself."

Rage has its disguises. I remember my first modest taste of confrontational demonstration, in downtown Oakland, California, October 20, 1967, at the end of what was called Stop the Draft Week. Several thousands gathered to clog the streets around the Oakland induction center, to prevent the draft system from launching new soldiers into the atrocious Vietnam War. Three days earlier, the cops had charged a crowd, clubbing viciously, spraying Mace, injuring many, singling out reporters and photographers. That day, the movement responded with mobile tactics. As the police charged, crowds feinted, retreated, ducked around corners, dragged trash cans, parked cars and potted trees into the intersections, burned draft cards in the faces of cops, played hide-and-seek. We pranced, we frolicked. No attacks on the police, but a pranking disobedience. When the police bullhorn blasted out, "In the name of the people of California . . . ," we chanted back in full-throated hubris, "*We* are the people." Che Guevara had just been killed in Bolivia, and spray painters took to the pavements with CHE IS ALIVE AND LIVING IN OAKLAND.

Thus dawned the movement phase known by the slogan "From Protest to Resistance." The war had been raging for years—two and a half years since the bombs started raining steadily on North Vietnam and U.S. Marines landed in the South. What I remember from the seedy morning streets of downtown Oakland is mainly fear and exhilaration. The exhilaration is the interesting part, springing from two sources: the joy of scampering away from the charging police, but also the vertiginous sense of freedom. We had cut loose from sluggishness, from the doldrums of submission, from common existence.

Joy wrapped our rage. Revolution is a festival of the oppressed, Lenin once wrote. (Festival of the depressed, my late friend, the talented movement journalist Andrew Kopkind, preferred to put it.) In Oakland the chant went up: "The streets belong to the people," meaning, of course, the thousands of us who blocked the streets, not the local people trying to get to work or the working-class draftees who had no patience for Berkeley riffraff who looked to them like draft dodgers. (In Mark Kitchell's documentary *Berkeley in the Sixties* there's a telling sequence shot outside the induction center, where a crew cut youth squares off to smash the face of a demonstrator who's trying to convince him to resist the draft.) We told ourselves that we were exhilarated because we were seriously obstructing the war effort by stalling induction for a few hours. But truly, madly, deeply, we were overjoyed because we felt we had broken on through to the other side of the ordinary, stirred things up, outfoxed the cops, seized power in our provisional zone. *We got away with it.* When Alameda County put seven organizers on trial for conspiracy—the Oakland 7—they couldn't get a jury to convict.

California wildness is easy to mock. This particular past was not only a foreign country, it was a carnival and a costume party. We were "freaks"—a positive label, in our book. Under the spell of Vietnam, logic and proportion had "fallen soggy dead"—so sang Jefferson Airplane. To put it another way, in the Bay Area of 1967, a freak show wasn't only a freak show. In the land of the Airplane, Janis Joplin, the Grateful Dead, the Hell's Angels and Haight-Ashbury—all meshing somehow with the Free Speech Movement and its political sequels—frolics made sense. But wildness was not restricted to California. That same week, Abbie Hoffman and a few friends performed an exorcism at the Pentagon, failing to levitate it while chanting "Out, demon, out," and more memorably, a breakaway antiwar demonstration numbering some 35,000 marched to the Pentagon and laid nonviolent siege overnight. "Remember kids, when you're out there smashing the state, don't forget to keep a smile on your lips and a song in your heart," in the words of an underground comic artist. For letterhead stationery, late SDS appropriated a published cartoon showing a bunch of kids scampering around the schoolyard as hapless Keystone Kops ran after them waving butterfly nets. Movement mobilizations were not only theater, they were farce, pranks, surrealism on stilts. Do good by having fun. *Get away with it.* If it feels good, do it. Empower yourself, we might say today.

The fun was in large part a façade—desperado revelry. In the lives of the movement's molten core, the late days of the sixties were consecrated to hallucinations. Writing these passages at a remove of more than three decades, in truth the feeling of pure rambunctiousness flows back to me—the élan, the sexiness, the thrill of steering through the white-water onrush of history on the strength of your feelings, however crazy. . . . There's nothing like the giddiness of a wild hope that you might just be able to force a victory—and even if in the end you may not prevail, the hell with it, at least here and now you can face down your separateness and fear, you can *live*. Juvenile rambunctiousness is nothing to apologize for: Whoever cannot make contact with the romance of youth has expired. How downright sad—how uncomprehending—that Apollonians overpaint the Dionysian colors with grayness! We were not having ourselves a time, we were submitting to—and at the same time mastering—the cascade of History. The recklessness was somehow a proof that it *was* History, and that we were up to it.

But the movement's fun in its late days was desperate. The fun tempered the rage—for a while—and when the fun wore thin, the rage sprang out, which proved disastrous. The jamboree of unbounded feeling roared straight ahead to the dark side. At bottom, rage was the argument for expressing rage. Feeling masqueraded as a political project—"raising the ante," "intensifying the struggle," "fighting fascism" or at the giddy heights, "revolution"—but really, feeling spoke for itself. By 1971, friends of mine justified smashing shop windows in downtown Berkeley on the grounds that the war was so horrible, they were filled with so much rage, they had to release it. "Power to the people" didn't make room for shopkeepers. Blocking the trucks in the Oakland streets, we seceded from our own people. No wonder we were despised even as the war we opposed was despised.

For a lesson on what guilt and rage can do when they go out for a spin, consider again the Weathermen, who hijacked the New Left, leaving millions of befuddled radicals staring at the wreck as if paralyzed at the scene of an accident. In 1969, after four fierce years of growing and increasingly militant protest against the war, there arose a hundred or so of the Weather warriors, breaking away from what they thought was a wimpy old student movement. These warriors decided that some kind of revolution was nigh and that the entire American people were the enemies of the righteous. They believed that they would win respect and recruits from the working-class young by toughening up during breaks from sex and drugs, that a hodgepodge of Third Worldist slogans was potent enough to justify all manner of violent actions. The Weathermen were prevented from committing the mass murders they were planning solely by the accident that one of their bombs blew up prematurely in an 11th Street townhouse in Greenwich Village, killing three of their own. Many of us who knew they were riding off the rails were demoralized and inhibited about opposing them. We failed to organize any alternative to them and their Stalinist-Maoist rivals. Nothing fruitful whatever came of their wild and muddled exercise in bad theater.

Just so, but on a grander scale and with far less mirth, the Black Panther Party hijacked the black liberation movement while intellectuals stared—impressed despite themselves, dumbfounded and thrilled. "Off the Pig!" "Free Huey or the Sky's the Limit!" "By Any Means Necessary!" The Panthers liked to take credit for serving breakfast to children—along with propagandistic slogan chanting—as if Free Huey chants were the necessary accompaniments to orange juice and toast. The Panthers specialized in insinuations of violence—sometimes retaliatory, sometimes not—while liberals were chastised (and chastised themselves) for looking askance at their threatening demeanor and paramilitary formations. Raising critical questions about their shoot-outs with police was very bad form. Guilt produced intimidation and silence. Weren't chief ideologue Huey Newton's proclamations banal? To say so would have been impolite. Weren't chairman Bobby Seale's declarations crude and fantastical? I remember sitting on a panel on radical action at Berkeley early in 1969, when a drunken Bobby Seale entered the back of the auditorium and started yelling incoherently. When the chair politely asked him to desist, Seale demanded, "Don't you know what they're doing to us?"—the all-purpose excuse. I remember Seale browbeating a woman for asking impertinent questions at a reading of Mao's Little Red Book. White radicals (including me, I'm ashamed to say) shut up because the principle of black leadership was sacrosanct. In the end, though some black politicians emerged from the rubble once they outgrew their romance with violence, precious little came of the party's armed bravado, their paramilitary gestures, shoot-outs and revolutionary posturing.

The Panthers had been resoundingly defeated by the police by the time the Symbionese Liberation Army came along, dressed up in military costume and claiming to act in the wrathful name of the oppressed, offspring of the fantasy that black prisoners were the vanguard of a coming revolution. Like the Black Liberation Army and other tiny squads, they went farther than most of the dying New Left liked in celebrating the white radical romance for black prisoners—the tougher, more audacious and cold-bloodedly murderous, the better. Nothing worthy whatever came of the Symbionese liberationists of the mid seventies—assassins of Oakland's first black superintendent of schools (responsible for a security system that the assassins construed as an invasion of children's freedom), kidnappers, murderers, most of them in turn killed by the Los Angeles police, winning them a reputation for martyrdom. Their obscurantism ("Symbionese"), vagueness ("Liberation") and chutzpah ("Army") were of a piece with the vileness of their tactics. Like the Latin American urban guerrillas from whom such gangs took inspiration, the soldiers drew down the wrath of the armed state and left nothing behind but blood.

Having missed the high tide of militancy, the SLA did not even try to convince large numbers of cadres that their way was the right way. Their language was like a secret handshake meant to boost morale. A few recruits would do, as long as they had guns and were ready to use them. Accordingly, SLA slogans were stupefyingly garbled. With no detectable grasp of political ideas, they spoke in self-parodying claptrap ("Death to the fascist insect that preys upon the life of the people"). This is the way people talk when they have no real following or any serious intention of organizing one. Only the SLA's actions made its words worthy of notice. Its soldiers embraced the lunatic theory that they could make their actions mean whatever they said by simply declaring they had big ideas and daring anyone to disagree with them. Not for them the moral requirement of making a reasonable case that their means might conceivably lead to desirable ends.

Recently, when SLA remnants went on trial, former Black Panther chairman and cofounder Bobby Seale was quoted as saying, "The SLA was a clear government setup to discredit the positive revolutionary movement we were leading." This is paranoid fantasy upon fantasy. As for Seale's "positive revolutionary movement," Hugh Pearson in *The Shadow of the Panther* amassed much evidence that Panthers cofounder Huey Newton was a maniacal tyrant, no "positive" fellow at all. To blame the government for the likes of the SLA in order to protect the glamorous Panther myth is historical fraud. Whatever the apostles of false innocence think, bad ideas do not require government agents. There were never more than a score of SLA "soldiers," but in its farcical, nightmarish way the SLA helped to inter the dreams of a decade.

Around now, you may be wondering whether I'm getting hung up on some bad old scenarios—a sort of negative nostalgia. What do these lurid cautionary tales have to do with you? This: I'm afraid that the temptation of going for broke is a perennial. Not only history and self-scrutiny tell me so. I also hear traces of the old recklessness in some of the globalization debates and in Green Party excitement about the spoiler potential amply demonstrated in the 2000 election. Whenever movements heat up, so does the temptation to raise the ante. May I offer a psychological hypothesis to make sense of something that seems otherwise senseless, namely, the payoff of unbridled emotion?

When guilt and rage drive action, you may be striving to wrestle your more sensible self into submission.

That's how it was for me and many of my friends when the militants took the initiative. We let them intimidate us. If you're built the way I was, your paralysis feels so painful you want to murder the doubter within you. All the worse when guilt diminishes you, plays on self-hatred, and invites your diminished self to surrender to priests or demagogues. The more you're hated the more you revel in the infantile feeling that you're getting the world to pay attention. Even if you elude the exhibitionist trap, guilt is more likely to lead to sour paralysis than useful action. For guilt is a destroyer—even of your own guilty self. It's a bludgeon wielded by one part of you against another.

Please also beware obsessions with past oppressions. The guilt-rage complex fuels self-righteousness for which reasons can always be found, but when guilt and rage slip their leash, they murder the future in the name of an unsalvageable past. In a culture of amnesia, the usual advice is, Remember. But memory carved in granite is best suited for tombstones. See also the Middle East just about any day, where everyone could benefit from a yet unwritten anthem called In Praise of Forgetfulness. Perhaps you've already noticed that the enragé faces backward. Memory fuels revenge, and revanchist politics are always destructive—which is to say, they are not really politics at all but a metaphysical fury to repeal the world.

The moral is to beware your rage against injustice, for when it gets out of hand (easy enough), it feeds on a rejection of some (possibly unjust) side of yourself. As for practical use, rage usually backfires. Manipulating guilt is an act of aggression, and usually those you assault will respond in kind, with resentment—even resentment of you for putting them on the spot. You may succeed in bludgeoning a few recruits into the club of guilt, but as the club grows, so does the club of its enemies. Spawning more defensive resentment, you've isolated yourself and increased the amount of harshness in the world. The healthy alternative to rage is indignation—anger because the world is unworthy of you at your best, but equipped with an edge of hope because you know, and let others know, that better is possible. The crimes and sins of the world are insults to your care and intelligence. When you're affronted by cruelty and injustice, you're not diminished—to the contrary, you're enlarged, because you've taken part of the world into yourself, something to be remedied. You want to change minds, so you don't burn bridges. Burning bridges is the route of the fundamentalist, who prefers the world purified but embattled, each pain a pleasure, each Antichrist a confirmation of Christ.

It's a delicate business, knowing where to draw the line between the guilt-rage cycle and the joyful energy, indignation and responsibility you rightly insist on (if not you and not now, who and when?). In my political life I've been at my best when I've known the difference, taken up fights with a plain sense that there's work to be done in good fellowship rather than stuck rage. Start with rage if you must, but don't stop there. Affirmation not only feels better, it does better, more consistent, more enduring work—it has more pride. Not guilt, but revolt: I am revolted; I can't bear what the world is becoming; it is not worthy of us.

5

█ **On Changing the World and Blowing It Up, or Compromising with the Compromised**

Dear ——,

Radicals of the Left aren't *especially* bad or stupid folks; the Right has its own crimes and errors. Yet one reason our errors get out of hand is that there's a market for bravado.

The Bohemian impulse to twit respectable folk, which once had been the luxury of tiny cultural vanguards, has gone into mass circulation. The postsixties consumer economy does a nice business in tools for self-expression, from fashion to communications. Declaring who you are, disgorging your emotions, producing spectacular rituals, doing what feels good in public—all this is central to our culture. In a political atmosphere, these impulses like to dress up in political motives. But, as I hope I've convinced you, if you needed convincing, self-expression is not a useful political guide, nor even a good aesthetic one. The artist—the modernist, anyway—toys

with his materials, indifferent to immediate consequence, creating his own audience if he succeeds—and if
the world does not comprehend, so much the worse for
the world. If he lets himself be governed by the reactions
he anticipates from an audience, his art is corrupted and
he is enslaved. It's in this spirit that Rilke, in the book
that is my model, advised the young poet to look to his
inward feelings.

What Rilke didn't address (he didn't need to) is the
question of what to do with feelings *in here* that, once
acted on, get tangled up with other people's feelings *out
there*, and often enough spur reactions that do not work
out so well. Militancy arouses the blood, but this cannot
be its justification, for activists are responsible for the
consequences of their acts. If antiwar militancy can take
credit for driving Johnson from office in 1968, it must by
the same token shoulder blame for nudging some voters
toward Nixon, who proceeded to extend the Vietnam
War for five years and expanded it to Laos and Cambodia, killing more than a million people, inflicting untold
miseries. Escalating militancy (in urban riots as well as
antiwar demonstrations) panicked enough voters to
abandon the Democrats, whom they couldn't trust to
stabilize the country, and turn instead to Nixon or
George Wallace. Meanwhile, sooner than opt for the
compromised liberal Hubert Humphrey, some on the
Left went for statewide Peace and Freedom tickets,
while many sat out the election altogether. I was one of
these high-and-mighty abstainers, declaring publicly
that the fates had it in for America: We were headed either to fascism or revolution. Such foolhardy relish for
the apocalypse! (Surely the dopiest left-wing position

before the election campaign of 2000.) Hardly anyone I knew voted for Humphrey. The possibility never crossed my mind.

More voting Democrats moved right than left, and carried the country with them. This wasn't the Left's intention, though here and there whispers could be heard: Bring on the deluge! Either way, the result was foreseeable—if you had a sense of where the country's center of gravity was. If you didn't, you could let yourself believe that the mood in Berkeley, California, or Cambridge, Massachusetts, or Madison, Wisconsin, or the upper West Side of Manhattan forecast the national mood. This was the revolutionary delusion—to extrapolate grand results from your acquaintances, to let the wish be the mother of all assessments. Against this intoxication, the practical activist looks at the world as it is, takes account of not-so-pleasant reactions, and is not surprised that the rising curve of opposition to war may well bring with it the rising curve of opposition to the movement opposing war.

This is the huge, disconcerting fact about the sixties. As demonstrations became more disruptive (or the police attacks on them did, a distinction often lacking in news reports), they signaled revolution to a population that, whatever its growing disaffection from the war, had zero or negative interest in revolution. After the Chicago Democratic Convention confrontation of August 1968, almost 40 percent of whites *who wanted U.S. withdrawal from Vietnam* thought the Chicago police had not used enough force. The antiwar movement was loathed more than any other group in the country. That those who hated the Left most were working-class whites who resented our privileges should come as no surprise. When they said, "It's a rich man's war and the poor people fight it," they were not in a mood to include us among their friends. Their own resentment led them to exaggerate. Most of us were not rich kids living off trust funds; we were upset that working-class kids would be fighting in Vietnam in our place; and we did what we could to publicize the class bias of the draft and to counsel vulnerable young men on resistance. Our doomed efforts to overcome class privilege, however sincere, did not make us many friends. That these young men were suspicious of us did not make them automatically virtuous, and sometimes they were racist. Nevertheless, shoving this bloc against the wall came at a high cost.

We had no idea how bad things could get. We felt—*I* felt—too young to care much about consequences. What catastrophic idiocy. How delicious it felt.

Perhaps the whole subject of elections bores you as it once bored me. Waiting in line to vote is so much stodgier, so much less fun than filling the streets and other colorful direct actions. But you had better pay close attention to election campaigns, for their outcomes will pay close attention to you and your prospects. However imperfect the choices, you will live with them, the boundaries of your results will be colored by them. So you can't afford to measure the good of an action by how much fun it is.

Speaking of elections, it may seem to you like Babylonian history to speak of a time when a tainted liberal spoke for the *right* wing of the Democratic Party. That the political weakling Hubert Humphrey, fatally implicated in the Vietnam War, deserves blame for his own defeat may seem obvious. Yet the pleasure of blaming the unsatisfactory is a luxury that activists cannot afford. What matters is results. We do not go looking for alibis. We cannot invent the world we are trying to change. We cannot disinvent unsatisfactory souls. Our purity of heart is no argument. (The poor who suffer most when we fail cannot afford to dine out on our purity of heart.) All we have at our disposal is our own action—not least, the campaigns that put people in power.

So Humphrey's chief primary opponent, Eugene McCarthy, pure of intention, does not escape judgment either. Having won the affection of millions, he failed to wring concessions from Humphrey during the fall campaign, and failed to rally his followers to cast votes for Humphrey that would have stood a decent chance of shutting down the war. The November 1968 vote was so close that a shift of 334,000 votes in three states with strong antiwar constituencies (California, Oregon and Wisconsin) would have cost Nixon his electoral majority and, under an infrequently used provision of the Constitution, thrown the decision into the House of Representatives, where a Democratic majority of state delegations would have put Humphrey in the White House.

What would Humphrey have done? Given that by 1968 most Democrats hated the war, there were good odds (though true, no guarantees) that he would have phased out the war—not expanded it for five more years under cover of peace talks, as Nixon did. Be as skeptical as you like about what remained of Humphrey's earnest liberalism after five years of sitting on Johnson's lap. You are still hard pressed to argue rationally that, had Humphrey ascended to the White House, he would have done anything like the damage Nixon did in Southeast Asia. But the movement was not reasoning so carefully. We were inflamed by Democratic betrayal—that was the bright-red glow in the foreground of our vision. We saw only the fatally tainted Humphrey; Nixon hardly existed for us except as a ghoulish retread from the fifties, a politician so obviously awful as to be an uninteresting enemy. Dumping the Hump was the visceral need. Negativity prevailed. So in all innocence—deep, sincere and myopic innocence, no less myopic for all our sincerity—we stood on the sidelines and stared, both helpless and deluded, as the country stumbled into an era we couldn't seriously imagine yet paradoxically thought (sometimes in brute fear, sometimes in perverse desire) inevitable. Republican rule swept in, coloring the political landscape, not least the Rehnquist court, down to this day.

In 2000, the same belief that the difference between Democrats and Republicans was insignificant led enough left-wing voters into Ralph Nader's column (with the unwitting help of Palm Beach County's otherworldly association, Jews for Buchanan) to tilt the election outcome to George W. Bush. Again, the result was foreseeable—indeed, foreseen by critics who warned of the risk that Bush would capitalize on Nader's campaign. Throughout the fall, as polls showed Gore and Bush neck and neck, Nader supporters either argued that the presidential outcome didn't matter (come Tweedledee or Tweedledum, corporations would win) or disputed that their votes would make a difference (claiming, on next to no evidence, that Nader would draw equal numbers of votes from Democrats and Republicans). Sometimes they claimed to be the angelic embodiments of principle, rising above mere practical considerations. Sometimes they resorted to their own practical arguments, advocating "strategic voting" for Nader in states where polls showed their votes wouldn't matter, oblivious of the fact that letting the polls make up your mind for you conditions a moral choice on the presupposition that polls are reliable (when in fact they were swinging all over the place in that campaign). When it suited him, Nader resorted to the pragmatic argument that enough Green voters in Washington State came out to vote to put Democratic Senatorial candidate Maria Cantwell over the top (by a slim margin of 2,229 votes), while refusing to acknowledge the equivalent argument about his gift to Bush in the case of Florida.

Green arguments swerved all over the map. Sometimes the Greens maintained that by running an independent campaign they would push Democrats to the left—though why running within the Democratic Party wouldn't be more effective toward that end was unclear. Why Democratic politicians wouldn't reason that they could pick up more voters on their right than the Greens would pick up on their left was equally unclear. More often, the Greens maintained that they were building their party for the long term—as if a tiny minority party stood any chance of displacing a major party in a constitutional winner-take-all system. They spoke stirringly of the long term, though the long term leads through many short terms. That much irreversible damage (to the environment, the economy, the courts, the strength of social supports for the poor) can be done during these short terms did not impress them.

One conclusion imposes itself: The Greens' claims vacillated with ease because in the end, their practical calculations before and after the fact were masks. Underneath, what Nader voters really wanted was to vent their feelings. They were angry at Clinton's compromises, angry at Gore's compromises, angry at the dissipation of the consumer and environmentalist movements. They wanted to have a frisky and untainted movement of their own. Their crusade was their purpose and their reward. The purity of their feelings matters so much to them they are still washing their hands of the consequences. Bush's foreign policy, his depredations against environmental and arms treaties, against labor, against working-class taxpayers, against civil liberties and so on do not weigh much with them. Their rhetoric makes it clear that they relish the spoiler role. This is narcissism wearing a cloak of ideals.

Consequences: There's no getting away from them. How disconcerting that ideals and passions are compatible with gross miscalculations! A giant boulder lies in the path of those who think they can find salvation by sprinting with pure hearts from point A to point B. The boulder was named by the great sociologist Max Weber in a 1918 speech to radical students quoted in my first letter. Weber declared that those who want to act morally face a stark choice between two "fundamentally differing and irreconcilably opposed" ways of thinking about ethical conduct: "an ethic of ultimate ends" (what you do is good when your goals are good, and the bad guys are to blame when they get in your way) and "an ethic of responsibility" (what you do is good when the foreseeable outcomes of your actions are good, outcomes you cannot disown regardless of intentions). There is no having your cake and eating it. The ethic he recommends is, of course, the ethic of responsibility. Are you groaning? I did, once.

Weber doesn't want to give the last political word exclusively to practitioners of Machiavellian calculation. He's more complicated than that. He knows that politics "takes both passion and perspective." He tips his hat to the truth "that man would not have attained the possible unless time and again he had reached out for the impossible." "Politics is made with the head," he acknowledges, "but it is certainly not made with the head alone." Still, he is a stoic. He wants us to arm ourselves "with that steadfastness of heart which can brave even the crumbling of all hopes." He warns that "he who seeks the salvation of the soul, of his own and of others, should not seek it along the avenue of politics, for the quite different tasks of politics can only be solved by violence," meaning the trampling of moral ends by immoral means. (Even had Weber taken up the nice possibility of nonviolence, he would have insisted pitilessly that nonviolence, being coercive, also played with the fire of immoral means to moral ends.) He concludes: "Only he has the calling for politics who is sure that he shall not crumble when the world from his point of view is too stupid or too base for what he wants to offer. Only he who in the face of all this can say 'In spite of all!' has the calling for politics."

Weber positively dares you to dismiss him—as I certainly did in my early twenties when I read these words for the first time. He is anti-inspirational. He goes out of his way to call politics "a strong and slow boring of hard boards." (The word *boring* just about tells the tale.) He sounds too goddamned *reconciled*. The light from a different world does not seem to reach him. In the sixties, I thought—wished—that he must be wrong because he was grim, gray and painful. Damn his logic, the hell with him and his argument! If I'd been pressed to argue the point, I would have claimed that radical action might just transform the circumstances, make the impossible somewhat more possible, clear a narrow path around the boulder. That was probably a rationalization. The passion spoke louder, that's the truth. Who had the time or taste for perspective?

The recoil to the movement's militancy in the late sixties began changing my mind. The Right's sweep to power—Nixon, Ford, Reagan, Bush I, Bush II, overriding the Carter and Clinton interruptions—changed my mind. The haplessness and self-enclosure of the Left—its marginality, its inability or refusal to break out of academic and interest-group ghettoes—changed my mind. I've seen nothing since to change it back.

I confess I was once partial to the image of upheaval: Having inherited a losing position in an unsatisfactory game, turn over the board! What I learned is that when the old game collapses, the pieces do not discriminate: they fall on innocent heads. The next game might well be worse. I learned to reject the conviction that the next game will be more favorable simply because it's the next. Recoil is not a poet's career problem, but it *is* an activist's, because the canvas on which an activist works is society, a vast, messy, interdependent whole. In the artist's studio, there's only room for one brush—yours.

In your solitude lies your exhilaration. In a movement, your brush has to work in harmony with others. If enough of you paint together, you imagine that *you are the people*—or worse, *God's* people. Ah, the ring of the words. But society is full of would-be artists with all their clashing desires. What is to be done about those inconvenient souls? At the dead end of this logic, they are expendable. Politics, like hell, is other people. In a world bound together by media, investment, migration and violence, consequences ripple outward far and wide. So in politics, you need to channel your impulses, frustrate your spontaneity, think as well as feel, settle for less than the ideal result, because you live alongside others, because they are the field of your action, because consequences count and history is unforgiving.

If you object (perhaps in the name of freedom of the will) that no one can really control other people's reactions, that overbearing fear of a terrible recoil is paralyzing, that you can talk yourself into passivity, I can only say you have a point. Endless passivity encourages the arrogant powers to think that they can get away with murder. Fear of failure becomes overwhelming, and weakness, self-fulfilling. You can overcalculate yourself into insensibility.

So be cautious, lest you become too cautious. I implore you: Think through your situation in all its particulars. Assess your actual strength unsentimentally. Consider the possibility that if you always compromise and your enemies don't, the center will keep edging away from you, but don't assume that a steadfast attachment to your uncompromising position will have the opposite effect. It's possible, but far from inevitable.

Bullheadedness doesn't prevail automatically. You may massage your soul but accomplish nothing else. Say what you think, but be thoughtful enough to see the virtue in an outcome that's not as good as you want but probably as good as it gets. Then get back to work—criticizing, mobilizing, organizing, listening, considering.

Political intellectuals, not only on the Left, have been especially stupid about the messy clash and coexistence of passions in a complex society—not just *this* fallen society but *all* modern society. The urge to set the world right tends (if you're not careful) toward an absolute passion. In the name of a rage against injustice, you want to cut through entanglements, obliterate hesitations, swarm over the field of action, mobilize your power against *their* power. In the intense heat of the struggle— by now a disembodied noun—the love with which you began melts away, leaving hatred and an abstract will to justice.

Sartre once knew the score. In his diabolical play *Dirty Hands*, the canny party chief Hoederer accuses the young Communist intellectual Hugo, who's been criticizing him for his compromised politics. "You are afraid to dirty your hands. Well, stay pure! . . . Purity is a fakir's idea, a monk's." Hoederer, though, is proud to have "dirty hands, up to the elbows. I plunge them in shit and blood . . ." He therefore cares about saving lives. As for Hugo, Hoederer says, "You don't love men. You love only principles. . . . If you don't love men, you can't fight for them." Hugo: "Why should I love them? Do they love me? . . . As for men, what interests me is not what they are but what they may become." Hoederer: "And I love them as they are. With all their dirty tricks and all their vices. I love them with their hot hands and their skin, the most naked of all skin, and their troubled looks and the desperate struggle they fight every day against death and anguish. For me, one man more or less counts in the world. It's precious. I know you well, mon petit. You are a destroyer. You detest men because you detest yourself; your purity resembles death and the Revolution of which you dream is not ours: you don't want to change the world, you want to blow it up . . . . An intellectual is not a real revolutionary, he's just good enough to be an assassin." Hoederer does not know that in fact Hugo's been sent by the party to assassinate him.

Hoederer has Hugo's number. When Hugo finally gets up the nerve to kill him, he doesn't even do it for political reasons, but out of misguided jealousy. All Hugo's nice reasoning turns out to be a flimsy façade for passion. Sartre's ironic eye is merciless. (It gets worse for poor harsh Hugo. We learn at the end, when Hugo has gotten out of jail, that the party line has changed and Hoederer in death has been refashioned as a martyr.)

Rage, the great simplifier, ever renews its promise to cleanse the earth in the name of purification. All manner of fundamentalists—Islamist, Christian, Jewish, Maoist, fascist—have their hearts set on destruction, while intellectuals pretty up their motives. Thirteen years after writing *Dirty Hands*, Sartre himself, introducing Frantz Fanon's *The Wretched of the Earth*, embraced anticolonial violence. Since the goal was absolutely and not relatively good, no cost in human life was too high, no vengeance unjustified. Were the circumstances different, Sartre would have deplored this line of thought as bad faith, dishonest because it is both blind to motives and myopic about consequences. The most intelligent people can be stupid that way.

So you see, it's not that I fail to understand your passion. The rapture of purism is a political aphrodisiac. It's precisely *because* I do know the feeling that I caution you: keep it under control.

6

■ On the Intricate Dance of
Outsiders and Insiders,
or Shouts Lead to Murmurs

Dear ——,

You protest that my fears leave you cold. You renounce any desire, hidden or otherwise, to blow up the world. You are a sweet person, genuinely committed to constructive change. You have left behind left-wing revolutionism—a creature of a dinosauric, prepostmodern age of absolutist fancies—in favor of a more modest and focused, indeed more constructive project: resisting the onward march of so-called globalization that enriches the world's rich and impoverishes the world's poor, pulverizes local differences, endangers the world's climate and the prospects of viable life. You stand with the human rights activists, the students against sweatshops, the organizers of unions and the indigenous people against resource marauders. Instead of rampant American-style market fundamentalism and diminished states, you want the best of Enlightenment universalism, the extension of social and economic rights everywhere. You affirm the right to be different as well as the right to be different differently, against those (such as Islamists) who insist that *their* difference is the only one permitted. Toward that end, you want grand but still imaginable goals, realizable step by step, even fit by start: global human rights, institutions of global justice (such as the International Criminal Court), the rich world doing more for and less against the poor world. You want, for example, to tax securities transactions (the so-called Tobin tax) a fraction of 1 percent to underwrite development aid. You want to phase out fossil fuel dependency in favor of renewable energy. You want to forgive much of the impoverished countries' debilitating debt, though without letting corrupt government elites off the hook. You want multinational corporations to ratchet up wages, working and environmental conditions. You're acutely aware of the particular and acute responsibilities of a nation whose elites, at least, are not only the prime beneficiaries of low resource prices but also the planet's prime polluters, global warmers and arms traders. Yet you have no illusions either that American corporations are particularly more benighted than European or Japanese corporations, or that countries lacking outside investment or trade are more "progressive" than those with it. Some may say they want an end to globalization but most want a more just version, a global New Deal. Now what?

The hard-core skeptic is not terribly impressed. To him you fairly beg to be dismissed when you clamor, say, against the World Bank and the International Monetary Fund. You are party crashers or worse—in wartime, some call you traitors. Thanks especially to the media penchant to focus on the wildest and woolliest in your company, you look like a pack of loudmouths and flat earthers, juvenile showboats and superannuated Left-overs, at best an irritating rabble of grandstanders who oversimplify complex problems that need expert man-agement. Some of the slogans in your crowd certainly sound simplistic, the remedies recklessly all or nothing, as in SHUT DOWN THE IMF AND WORLD BANK and DE-FUND THE FUND. The chanters in your crowd believe the World Bank and IMF so discred-ited by rule of the wealthy, so punitive toward the poor and ruinous toward environmental sanity, these institu-tions cannot be repaired. They think the most construc-tive thing they can say is STOP.

What you must tell the skeptics is that the movement that surfaced in Seattle, November 1999, is a whirlwind, and the constructive side of a whirlwind is sometimes hard to see. Stridency distorts. Slogans by definition are simplistic. Slogans are meant to stir the souls of advo-cates, however much they irritate more cautious or com-placent souls, who proceed to denounce the sloganeers with their own slogan, "Simplistic!" After all, a bumper sticker is not an argument. It is an impetus that says, Change the agenda! The wisest movements know this; but movements are not built solely by the wise.

You have another high-wire act to perform. You must be better than your best critics. You're uneasy, and rightly so, with the blowhard who thinks in insults and sound bites—even your own blowhard. When your crit-ics deplore some of your tactics and proposals, you're willing to take another look. You know not all commo-tion is helpful, for a necessary is not a sufficient condition; the wrong kind can undermine constructive efforts; the tactic or proposal that galvanizes discussion and serious reform efforts at the beginning of an organizing campaign may cause a campaign in progress to stall later on. But after all this recognizing is done, you must insist, against your critics, that major political change often— no, usually—requires social commotion whose heat must then be contained and focused.

This is why successful protest movements require two types of activists working (whether they know it or not) in tandem. There are the outsiders, usually young, moralistic, committed to confronting the powers that be with evidence of errors, sins and crimes. You're among them. You believe that what you lack is not arguments but power, and that your deepest power, your prime resource, is the power to obstruct the smooth workings of the prevailing machinery. Outsiders like you raise their voices, commit civil—and sometimes not so civil—disobedience. Insiders, by contrast, are usually my age— professionals, mainly academics and lawyers. They are older, more accomplished, lovers of order who tend not to raise their voices. They are familiar with the ways of bureaucracy. They write memos. They believe themselves to be mastering the art of the possible. They may not be such fun to hang out with. Argument and deal making are their forms of demonstration. They are comfortable managing and being managed.

Some mutual respect between outsiders and insiders might go a long way. Insiders need to get used to your untidiness, curb their dismissiveness and listen for the justice in the clamor. You, though, would be well advised to make as much sense as possible, to curb your nihilists, to make some manageable demands and win some small victories, to bring your more thoughtful, articulate people to the fore and not punish them for competence. Don't assume that every word uttered by your team makes sense, or that every word uttered by the other team is worth dismissing strictly because of the source. Your campaigns to improve sweatshop conditions in the south of the world have shown an exemplary sophistication. As in the campaigns of the mid eighties to get universities and other investors to sever connections with companies doing business in apartheid South Africa, knowing your stuff pays off in concrete change.* So too with human rights campaigns pioneered by Amnesty International, with Greenpeace's campaigns against whaling, the Rainforest Action Network's campaigns against corporate abominations, international efforts to abolish land mines and forgive African debt and many others. In all of these, outsiders have pushed, encouraged and

---

*The present-day campaign to divest from Israel, however, is full of false parallels. In South Africa, a single illegitimate regime represented a minority that ruled tyrannically over the majority, whereas Israel is a democracy, however flawed, and the problem in the Middle East is to bring about two legitimate regimes ruling two distinct nations neither of which occupies the other. In another case of misplaced parallels, a Europe-based campaign calls on academic associations to sever relations with Israeli academics. This campaign too demonizes Israelis, many of whom support a land for peace arrangement that would end the unjust occupation of the West Bank and Gaza. Activists should always be leery of any claim that assumes that all the righteousness is to be found on one side. Thorough appraisals of Middle East history show plenty of blame to go around.

strengthened insiders—though the insiders haven't always been pleased to have the help.

Insider and outsider impulses sometimes coexist and war in the same breast. Some outsiders are former insiders—Daniel Ellsberg, for example, the career Pentagon official who, in 1971, released the Pentagon Papers on Vietnam to the *Washington Post* and *New York Times*, risking a long jail sentence and reprisals by President Nixon's operatives. Ellsberg proceeded to cross the line, devoting himself for decades to civil disobedience against American nuclear policy. Outsiders may in turn become insiders. Tom Hayden, for example, principal author of SDS's *Port Huron Statement*, sought and held state office in California and became a powerful voice in education and environmental policy there for a quarter of a century—much longer than he spent as a student and community organizer and planner of demonstrations. Don't accuse ex-outsiders of selling out, a charge that is not only smug, drenched as it is in moral superiority, but self-defeating, since it foreswears influence and regresses to the Manichaean presumption that all will be better when *all* your outsiders displace *all* the other side's insiders—a dubious proposition trailing Leninist fumes—or when no more insiders exist (a hallucination). Rather than hallucinate or plot coups, it behooves outsiders to contact insiders, argue with them, learn something from them, challenge them and resist the all-or-nothing temptation to demonize them. Equally, it behooves insiders to listen to outsiders, not just to cool them out. Any real reformer greets you and your friends as useful allies.

In America, organizations of all sorts—governmental, corporate, professional, what have you—harbor dissidents alongside the usual time servers and toadies. The dissidents are outnumbered, of course, but post–New Left, post–Ralph Nader they're strong enough to support a culture of whistle-blowing that, for all the rollbacks of recent decades, still flourishes. Organizations don't always have the power of compulsion that they used to—or crave. Top-down hierarchy has lost some of its authority. American culture still exalts the rugged individualist over the team player. As historian Michael McGerr has argued, individualism thrives partly because, with the economic instability of the seventies and eighties, employers opted out from their responsibility to their employees, who in turn discovered that they could draw on a range of resources—religion, spirituality, consumerism, a host of "lifestyle" emphases—to elevate their own needs over those of their organizations. So conscientious objectors abound and radical outsiders will run into sympathetic insiders in many surprising places.

As an outsider, you may resent this—I know I have—but one of your prime functions is to improve the clout of insiders. Your shouts lead to their murmurs. Get to know these people. They might have useful advice, not least on where to focus your energies—issues that you might find leverage with, allies whom you might unearth, victories that might be attainable. You don't want to tie yourself in knots to conform to their agenda, but odds are, they'll have something useful to tell you. And they need to hear from you about outsider sentiment, need to be reminded of what is at stake. In short, you need each other. For you are undertaking the time-honored, indispensable mission of democratic crowds: to crack a wrongheaded consensus, to energize actual and potential reformers on the inside, to polarize opinion and goad laggards, to precipitate public debates that have been suppressed by establishments or pursued, if at all, only by experts in closed rooms where inertia and groupthink overwhelm intelligence.

Cultivate this necessary division of labor: Outsiders set agendas and insiders roll up their sleeves and get to work, possibly better funded, possibly more urgently than before. Under the right conditions, agendas and reform prospects expand. Thus in the early sixties, when civil rights demonstrators brought the country to a boil, demanding voting rights and an end to segregation, they not only inspired a wave of antidiscrimination laws but stirred a growing concern with economic inequality. Washington insiders were able to devise and implement the War on Poverty while outsiders went on extrapolating from their victories, generalizing equal rights demands to many minority groups and to women. Insiders will sniff at misinformation and bad reasoning. Still, the enlightened, problem-solving experts gain a hearing inside the halls of power precisely because there is clamor outside, even if those who clamor are stronger on critique than on proposals. In this way, the causes of rain forest preservation, AIDS drugs, alternatives to dams and better working conditions in Third World factories have all benefited from the nonviolent campaigns of recent years.

It would seem that, thanks to globalization reformers, the language of the debate has changed drastically—indeed, there *is* a debate. Consider the following diagnosis of today's global economics. "Tremendous power has flowed to the people entrusted to bring the gospel of the market to the far corners of the globe . . . the culture of international economic policy in the world's most powerful democracy is not democratic." The author of these words is not a window-smashing anarchist from the far northwest but the quintessential insider, former World Bank chief economist Joseph Stiglitz, writing in the April 17, 2000, issue of *The New Republic*, concurrent with demonstrations at the World Bank and the International Monetary Fund. Because sensible outsider passions have surged up in recent years, reform-minded insiders such as Stiglitz have gained larger and more attentive audiences. Many, including the ordinarily dismissive *New Republic*, pay attention to such words because of the shouts in the streets. Stiglitz later wrote that until the movement developed, "there was little hope for change and no outlets for complaint. . . . *Some* of the protestors went to excesses; *some* of the protestors were arguing for higher protectionist barriers against the developing countries, which would have made their plight even worse. But despite these problems, it is the trade unionists, students, environmentalists—ordinary citizens—marching in the streets of Prague, Seattle, Washington, and Genoa who have put the need for reform on the agenda of the developed world."

You will challenge me now, and you should. You wonder whether kinder, gentler establishment rhetoric is anything more than a cover for business as usual. On principle, you're right to suspect a bit of a shell game. When the powerful learn to speak street dialect, one thing they're hoping to do is cool out the clamor. That's the way of the shrewder colonial. So be wary too. Inquire deeply. Watch for unmet promises and overly cheery statistics. Don't take declarations of deep commitment at face value. Show me an institution that doesn't profess abiding commitment to the progress and prosperity of the wretched of the earth and I'll show you an institution that hasn't paid its public relations bill.

But don't let your skepticism turn corrosive. Be open to signs of improvement. However mixed the motives, reform does take place—partly because of you. As one debt relief activist, Mara Vanderslice, wrote in a 2002 e-mail to supporters, the global campaign for Third World debt relief, after several years of nonviolent demonstrations, "more than doubled school enrollment in Uganda, provided three extra years of schooling for Honduran children and vaccinated half a million children against preventable diseases in Mozambique. Resources have been leveraged to fight against HIV/AIDS in Mali, Senegal, Uganda and Cameroon." But don't just oppose depredations, debate alternatives. Pay heed to the intellectuals striving to formulate varieties of just, sustainable globalization as alternatives to the destructive kind now in play. Sophisticated people know that antiglobalization is a fantastical conceit, something like antigravity, the point rather being to *reform* globalization, move it toward equality, not just support nativist rebellions (which are as likely to be fascistic as not, à la the French National Front and American anti–U.N.

militias). When you feel disheartened by the raggedness and ignorance on display, remember that movements are not centralized think tanks that adopt and enforce party lines. They are mélanges, dispersed, polycentric and fluid, their positions all over the lot. Remind insiders of this. Movements frustrate our hopes for orderly reason, and sometimes do more than frustrate them—they blast them apart. But don't let the movement's sloppiness distract you from its strength—and indispensability.

Insiders will sniff at radical declarations even if they approve of some outsider sentiments. They have no illusions that globalization can be swept away or global institutions dispensed with. Because the World Bank makes loans to projects that spread noxious chemicals, displace local farmers with gigantic dams and uproot sustainable agriculture in favor of growing crops for export, they still do not harbor illusions that the poor of the world can dispense with a World Bank altogether. Because the International Monetary Fund has increased human suffering on several continents in behalf of reckless privatization and the slashing of social safety nets does not mean that flat abolition is the remedy. Because the absolutist utopians in charge of the prosperous north of the world think markets solve all problems does not mean that markets can be discarded. The remedy for market fundamentalism is not antimarket fundamentalism. We've been down that grim road before.

You may be wondering whether I intend to go on blithely in this vein, as if the world hadn't changed when the hijacked airliners slammed into the World Trade Center and the Pentagon on September 11. Our discussion, like many others nowadays, would seem to require an asterisk. Isn't totalitarian Islamism, with its penchant for apocalyptic violence, a force in the world that demands new thinking, new action, new priorities?

You're right to fear that the momentum of the globalization reform movement up through September 10, 2001, was gravely interrupted. Some activists lost heart. Others were diverted into opposing one or another element of the "war on terror"—not always wisely. Yet even as murderous networks mobilize to slaughter more Americans, the globalization reform movement is not going away, nor does it deserve to—which is not to say that its prospects extend ever onward and upward or that the forces arrayed against it (not least the movement's own fundamentalist tendencies) are trivial, or that our movement colleagues are predestined to make sense because, even if they do not talk the talk of the angels, they at least take sides against the devils we share. Even if it isn't always clear exactly which are the right policies to pursue, the problems addressed by reformers are enduring and morally compelling.

You wonder what is to become of these problems in the midst of terror and counterterror, the promise of unending war, unending attention *to* war, and a shrug from politicians and media to the effect that global equity and human rights are all very nice but we have more urgent business now and in the foreseeable future. True enough, most Americans may feel now and for extended periods to come that terrorism is the clearest and most present danger, and that the diffuse war on terrorism—or on one or another rogue state—is the more compelling cause. Those of an activist temperament may feel impelled to protest against a war disturbingly vague and reckless in its targets. The antiwar impulse may for a time eclipse the globalization and human rights concerns. (To make matters worse, some knee-jerk leftists get their frameworks grotesquely muddled and hallucinate that al-Qaeda's murderers are trivial criminals or even "objectively" anti-imperialist guerrillas, when in fact they are the advance army of a would-be counterempire hoping to restore a bygone caliphate and lacking the slightest interest in improving life for most of the world.) The world is so interlocked that urgency about the Middle East imbroglio can also interfere with action on general north-south questions. In April 2002, globalization demonstrators lost the spotlight to pro-Palestinian demonstrators in Washington, D.C., whose strident slogans, sometimes with an anti-Semitic tinge, were fresher and more exotic in the eyes of the press.

Continuing terrorist attacks on American soil would surely undermine the cause of globalization reform, fear not being the most serviceable emotional climate for reform. So here as in other respects, the open-ended operations of a terrorist army committed to attacks on Americans, not to mention an open-ended war on terrorists or tyrants like Sadaam Hussein, would widen the breach between Americans and the rest of the world. However cosmopolitan, you are not exempt from the circumstances of your society, and ought to acknowledge that terrorists are in the distinction-denying business, do not inspect their victims' credentials and do not care whether the people they murder are janitors, environmental activists, oil company executives—or even American citizens.

You may find yourself in the surprising position of agreeing with some of what your antagonists say. Don't worry about it. Even should you agree with them on one issue or another, you will still want to fend off the autocratic impulses of the party in power. You will want to declare your independence of intimidation from the likes of Attorney General John Ashcroft. You must not let up: Wartime is no time to squander ideals of justice and liberty, not logically, not historically. (The cause of racial justice got a big boost during World War II and Vietnam.) To the contrary, patriotism entails defense not only of people and airspace but also equal rights to life and liberty. If America is not just a territory but a house of values, what is patriotism if it does not entail readiness to sacrifice toward the greater good? Why cede the monopoly on patriotism to those who wave flags while cheerfully subsidizing the oil-exporting tyrannies? Is it a supreme act of patriotism to swell the riches of billionaires, to boost subsidies for agribusiness, to subsidize the moving of electronic corporate headquarters offshore to tax havens, when police and firefighters cannot afford to live in the cities they protect?

7

▦ On Our Own Character Question, or Uses of Discipline

Dear ——,

I've been writing so far mainly about styles of action. You confess that an unavoidable question is gnawing at you, and I confess back that it just as unavoidably gnaws at me—which is no reason to avoid it and every reason to raise it. Here goes: To perform the right action, what kind of person do you have to be? What kind of person do you *want* to be? Are you *willing* to be? To get to the nub of the problem, how fanatical do you want to be? How many meetings are you willing to go to? What are you willing to sacrifice? You think we've scraped up against dilemmas so far, but this one is a doozy. It's our equivalent of what popular politics has come to call "the character question"—a euphemistic evasion, since the relation between private and public life isn't obvious. In our case, though, the character question cuts to the quick. What kind of people are we, what kind of people must we be, if we are to accomplish what we need to accomplish?

For years I've been struck by what seems to be a systematic imbalance in the achievements of the Left and Right. Survey after survey on a vast range of issues consistently demonstrates that more Americans take left-of-center than right-of-center positions—whether on controlling fossil fuels, on bolstering equal rights of women and (on most but not all issues) social minorities, on court appointments, on progressive taxation, on public responsibility for health care, on deregulation, on protecting nature and on and on. Yet on most of these matters most of the time, for some quarter century now, accomplishments belie the balance of sentiments. The Right either prevails or owns the issue or blocks the Left's initiatives. Somehow the Right magnifies its strength. Somehow the Left diminishes its own. Whether the president is a Republican or a Democrat, the process is predictable (though the difference remains large, whatever Ralph Nader may think). How did it happen, this vast success of the antigovernment, fundamentalist, procorporate, nationalist-to-jingoist movement that after decades in the wilderness elected Ronald Reagan in 1980 and has controlled much of the government and political debate ever since? What does the Right know or do that the Left does not—or more to the point, who *is* the Right that the Left is not? And what can be done about it?

It is no trivial dimension of this victory that the Republican Party belongs to its right wing and nevertheless wins elections—not least the presidency. The Republicans win Congress, or when they lose, prevail anyway.

They win state houses and governorships. Thanks to their control of local politics, they preside over reapportionment and tilt Congress rightward. They appoint Supreme Court justices, and the lower judicial ranks too.

In recent times it surely has not escaped your notice in particular (though our media generally consider this old and minuscule news) that in 2000, George W. Bush was supported by a minority of American voters—not even taking into account the Florida debacle, which left Bush in possession of that state's twenty-five electoral votes, even though incontestably a majority of Florida voters entered their voting booths intending to vote for Al Gore. Incontestably too a company hired by Secretary of State Katherine Harris had purged the voting rolls of many legitimate black voters falsely accused of felony records. This is not the place to review the whole skein of appalling events that ushered Bush into the White House, but surely you will recall the infrastructure of scandal. The appalling events that made up the 2000 coup d'état were not just random, disconnected oddities. Their underpinnings—their necessary conditions—were long prepared for. After years of ground-level political work, the Republicans had placed legions of powerful figures on the ground, all in position to roll up their sleeves in any contingency. At the state level were Florida's governor, Jeb Bush, Secretary of State Harris and a legislature that during the post–election day imbroglio was poised to appoint its own slate of electors pledged to Bush, whatever Florida's voters intended or state courts decided, had the U.S. Supreme Court—normally respectful to a fault of state courts—not intervened with its grotesque decision yanking the decision about vote counting away from the Florida courts. If all the tiers of Florida power were not enough, in the end the 2000 election came down to a Supreme Court majority under a chief justice who, in 1964, was a Goldwater speechwriter denouncing anyone who would "compel children to attend certain schools for the sake of so-called integration."

So how did it happen that after the sixties, the Right overcame its weaknesses, entrenched itself and proceeded to dominate American politics? There's no single answer; I'll mention only a few of the more important. Since the late sixties, when Kevin Phillips tutored Nixon on "the emerging Republican majority," the Right has mastered wedge issues, driving apart elements of the New Deal Democratic coalition by deftly using that wrecking ball of wrecking balls, race. The Left's major institutional base—labor—crumbled, numbering (at this writing) barely more than one-eighth of the workforce. In the eyes of the more prosperous, the Right has been able to equate liberty with property; in the eyes of the less prosperous, all politics is equally corrupt or "irrelevant," so they do not mobilize. The Right has disproportionate access to the airwaves. Republicans dominate the small states, which the Constitution grants disproportionate voting strength in the Senate. The American population has gravitated southward and westward, away from New Deal solidarities. For its part, the academic Left, whose numbers were not trivial, spent an inordinate amount of its time and energy marching on the English department while the Right descended on Washington. The cultural Left in and around the academy, convinced that deconstructing the work of other intellectuals is the most important work in the world (without any irony about how self-serving this assumption is), was and remains preoccupied with theoretical niceties to which the question of who wields political power—namely, the question of whether Democrats or Republicans take the White House or Congress—seems largely irrelevant.

For now, I want to talk about one factor that doesn't normally get its due: the discipline gap. A bright line runs from the Orange County, California, John Birchers of the fifties to the Young Americans for Freedom of the sixties to the heartland evangelicals of the seventies to the Reaganites of the eighties, all the way up to the Republican squads organizing stormy demonstrations at Florida recounting offices in 2000. The Right wins the great game of organization—and in a mass democracy, that means the great game of politics. Our side is antiauthoritarian and pluralist to the point of separatism; we value differences and identity factions. We are fractious to the detriment of unity, but consider the price well worth paying. We are not quite sure how we feel about winning, anyway—isn't that a synonym for selling out? We like to argue about the political significance of movies and TV shows, not about the politics of pensions and living wages. The fanatics of the Right get up early and stay up late. Laying claim to reason and the idea of a universal truth, they believe in submerging differences for the sake of victory. Though they purport to value laissez-faire above all other values, they harbor no ambivalence about winning. Toward that end, they take instructions. They sit through meetings. None of this makes them insuperable, but it does make them the team to beat. And the Left will not beat them until it is just as serious—yes, just as fanatical—about winning.

The discipline gap stems from an existential imbalance. The Right believes in power, order, discipline and hierarchy. It takes to these values unbegrudgingly and unambivalently. It concentrates on getting and holding power. It is not conflicted about issuing marching orders, mobilizing its people—to meet, to vote, to lobby. About political power it is not ambivalent (except for the small libertarian wing of the Right). It may distrust big government, or say it does, but it trusts that it can serve its constituents by seizing control of precisely that government—talking about unity while acting to protect the wealthy, deepen inequality, deregulate markets, support conservative culture, enforce America's global reach and boost the military and security apparatus.

Now consider the ideological Left, the one that clusters around universities, intellectuals and cultural institutions, cherishes individual spunk, cultural style, racial, ethnic and sexual distinctness. This Left *is* ambivalent— as a matter of style, almost as a matter of principle. Many of its partisans are ambivalent even about participating in politics, which they see across the board—with some reason—as corrupt and "irrelevant." This Left considers its enemy to be deeply rooted historical forces that, as it happens, public consensus supports—capitalism, militarism, sometimes industrialism—all in all, The System. But The System is not terribly susceptible to political contests. The Left despises the political party that most of its constituents vote for. In the election seasons of recent years, much of the cultural Left swerved to Ralph

Nader and the Greens, who cannot win statewide let alone national contests but whose spoiler potential has been vividly demonstrated. Much of this Left actively disbelieves in discipline. It resists concentrating its energies. Its activists are fragmented, issue by issue, constituency by constituency. Not only would they rather be right than president, they would rather be right than collaborate. As Republicans parachuted officials, lobbyists and cadres into Florida to stop the local vote counts, it was hard to get the Left even to demonstrate against electoral cheating.* (I know; I tried.)

Let me put it to you bluntly. The Right wants power more than the Left does, organizes more fiercely to achieve it and therefore has an essential advantage in seeking it. On the Right are the Leninists of our time—ruthless, resolute, blunt. On the Left are more complicated, less disciplined folks with multiple, contradictory drives— purity, self-expression, guilt, resentment *and* power. The Left gets out-organized. Issue by issue, the causes of the Right are unpopular but their politics owns institutions.

Proof of this imbalance is evident if we contrast the history of the Right over the past half century with that of the Left. Younger historians have been usefully recti-

---

* One such Republican endeavor to shut down the vote count in Miami-Dade County was memorably welcomed by columnist Paul Gigot in the *Wall Street Journal* as a "bourgeois riot." Were the media "liberal" as charged, there might be one pundit somewhere who would have issued a call for an equivalent left-of-center action. No one did. Instead, much Democratic nervousness was expressed at the prospect that Jesse Jackson might organize demonstrations, a prospect the Gore campaign intervened to abort.

fying our picture of the sixties (including my own), reminding us that the roots of the conservative revival and the Reagan reaction lie there, little as activists grasped the fact at the time. Historian Lisa McGirr has written (in *Suburban Warriors*) of the zealots, the John Birchers, evangelicals and antitax libertarians of Orange County in southern California who started out in the fifties and succeeded in taking over the Republican Party of California, nominating Barry Goldwater for president in 1964, then electing Ronald Reagan governor of California in 1966. Even before the backlash from the civil rights, student and antiwar movements and before the counterculture and feminism gave them national resonance, they knew what they wanted—a rollback of communism and a shrinking of the welfare state. They were—using the word neutrally—fanatics. They opened their homes for meetings, showed propaganda movies, knocked on doors, passed around petitions and organized more meetings. They used bridge clubs, coffee klatches and barbecues. They thought globally and acted locally—boy, did they. They flocked to meetings on minor matters so that after years of work they might—to take an actual example—eventually choose an Orange County school superintendent who in 1963 declared the United Nations a topic unfit for classroom discussion. Their programs might have been vague or self-contradictory or factually challenged, but they were relentless and focused.

The activists of the John Birch Society, the Christian Anticommunist Crusade and other such groups fumed against the New Deal and wimpy, crypto-Communist softness in Washington not because they were victims of liberalism but because they were beneficiaries with moral passion to spare. They were winners, possessed of organizational skills: military-industrial staff, aerospace engineers, technical writers, doctors, dentists, military officers and army wives. They reveled in American dreams, felt entitled to American comforts, and it was precisely because of their entitlements that they feared enemies at their gates. In Orange County and other Sunbelt boom zones, they found fundamentalist ministers, anti-Communist lecturers (not least, movie stars) and bookshops to steel their nerves, grace their platforms and stoke their apocalyptic imaginations.

Brimming with confidence, these activists didn't mourn when they lost—they redoubled their efforts. Conservatives combined a doomsday pessimism (Communists, one worlders and secular humanists were taking over the world) with a furious optimism of the will (they could turn the tide). Insinuating their way into the Republican Party, Orange County cadres connected nicely with national right-wing networks who shared their preoccupations. More than one million people donated money, mostly in small sums, to the Goldwater campaign of 1964. Orange County conservatives and the draft-Goldwater movement received large financial infusions from right-wing businessmen such as Walter Knott (of the eponymous Berry Farm) and Carl Karcher (of Carl's, Jr. hamburgers). Goldwater was crushed—the wake of the Kennedy assassination was not their moment—but the warmer, fuzzier Reagan gubernatorial campaign arose from the rubble, and the rest is history. The progress of right-wing organizing—from the self-motivating avatars of a "Christian Republic" in the fifties to the Goldwaterites to the Christian Right activists of the late sixties and early seventies (many of them still hard at work)—seems clear enough in retrospect.

Ideologically, conservatives feel no ambivalence about authority. Wrote sponsor William F. Buckley, Jr., about the founding meeting of Young Americans for Freedom that he hosted at his Sharon, Connecticut, estate in 1960, "What was so striking in the students who met at Sharon is their appetite for power." F. Clifton White, who dreamed up Goldwater's grassroots campaign, learned his organizing tactics fighting Communists in the American Veterans Committee after World War II. He put together "cells"—a tactic he later deployed in taking over the Republican Party and converting the irregulars of Citizens for Goldwater-Miller into a fighting force that would thrive beyond their election day defeat. In later decades, the Christian Coalition would do the same. Top right-wing activist Grover Norquist hangs Lenin's portrait in his Washington living room and is in the habit of citing Lenin approvingly: "Probe with bayonets, looking for weakness."

The activists of the Right are, above all, practical. They crave results. They are not terribly interested in pure parties or theoretical refinements, not even in ideas or morals as such. Once the Christian Right decided to launch out of their churches and work the political arena, they preferred actual political and judicial power to private rectitude. To agree on a few central themes— military power, deregulation, tax cuts, tort reform, cultural rollback on abortion, gay rights and affirmative action—was enough. From Reagan's first term onward, they knew what to do with power when they acquired it.

Rarely did conservatives indulge in pipe dreams of deliverance by third parties. Even after the Goldwater debacle of 1964, no less a fanatic than Walter Knott was able to say, "I think that you have to work through a party. . . . [I]f you don't, you would be pretty ineffective."

When it comes to political parties, the Right is immensely disciplined—and its labors were repaid over the course of decades with a power grip over the Republican Party. On intellectual and journalist fronts, to boost its confidence and legitimacy it built its own institutions. It cultivated intellectuals and journalists, establishing a reputation for intellectual seriousness, rewarding epigones, cultivating careers such as that of the deceitful David Brock (he of *The Real Anita Hill*, Troopergate and other spurious Clinton-era exposés). Read Brock's confession, *Blinded by the Right*, to get a feel for that world. From the seventies onward, their tycoons and foundations subsidized the written word. They bought newspapers in the two major cities—the *Washington Times* and the *New York Post*. They subsidized magazines from the high end to the low. They rewarded their intellectuals with positions at think tanks (American Enterprise Institute, Heritage Foundation, Cato Institute, Manhattan Institute and others). They paid writers (among them Charles Murray and Dinesh D'Souza) to write sloppy but influential books, then bankrolled publicity for them. They subsidized brutal, meretricious journalism—propaganda is more like it—to undermine Bill Clinton's center-left efforts. For the benefit of ambitious young men and women, they spawned a whole little world of journals and law firms, political consultantships and fellowships, thick with possibilities for promotion and self-promotion, glory and wealth. In Washington, the Left could barely dream of such career opportunities. Instead, for a power-and-glamour grid, the Left had Hollywood and popular music, promising more money but much less immediate political influence.

The difference runs deeper than strategy: it's a profound difference of identity, of social character. The Left stands for hanging loose, the Right for tight control. The Left is Bohemia, the Right is headquarters. I knew hundreds of New Leftists, but in the course of a decade I don't think I encountered more than half a dozen who had the personalities for strong political careers—the patience, self-sacrifice, willingness to calculate what is winnable, toleration of small talk, interest in people, capacity to size up people's strengths and weaknesses and to make deals. New Leftists were undisciplined, unruly, talky, frequently narcissistic, ambivalent about politics in the first place. For myself, I would rather have written poetry than knocked on doors in poor neighborhoods. My friends left novels half written and took to documentary film, while right-wingers become lawyers and bankers.

Temperamentally as well as ideologically, we were anarchists. I don't mean this in the strict sense, against governments as a matter of principle, but as a matter of practice, how we lived and worked. Don't take the hand-me-down Marxist rhetoric too seriously—the New Left's spirit was bottom up, autonomous, self-governing. Here is the stark difference between the Old and New Lefts: The Old, in Leninist, Stalinist or Trotskyist variants, was at ease with righteous authorities, while the New, despite flirtations with Fidel Castro, Che Guevara,

Ho Chi Minh and Mao Tse-tung, imagined these worthies to be guerrilla fighters, bearded antibureaucrats, not the high-handed (and in the latter two cases, murderous) bosses they were. Only the soft wing of the New Left (and make no mistake, the soft outnumbered the hard) could have generated the slogan "Question Authority." Not surprisingly, left-of-center foundations such as Ford, MacArthur and Rockefeller are devotedly localist. They want to empower community groups and ethnic communities more than subsidize think tanks or publishing houses. "Think Globally, Act Locally" is not a slogan of the Right.

How we mistrusted power, including our own! Recruiting leaders was hard. (I, a newcomer, was elected president of SDS in 1963 because none of the other four candidates, each of whom was experienced, was willing to serve.) During the mid sixties, when Students for a Democratic Society was mushrooming, embattled by the FBI, the press and the Justice Department, it abolished its presidency and vice-presidency in favor of "secretaries." Imagine it! At the very moment when we were becoming a national political force, the very thought of legitimate power unnerved us. Leadership was supposed to rotate (except in organizations run by people of color, where authoritarianism was excused). Power was supposed to be "local" and "community-based," horizontal, not vertical. Later, feminists too discovered that natural leaders automatically met with rancor, resentment and barely disguised envy. Talent often was questioned, viewed as a disguise for that old dreadnought, power.

I'm guessing that you will have brushed up against this automatic suspicion of power too. (Suspicion is why

Foucault is a demigod in the curriculum.) You and I are alike this way: We prefer small affinity groups to big unwieldy organizations. We are quarrelsome and frolicsome. You and I don't scheme for months and years to take over depleted Democratic parties or nominate our own candidates as Democrats. When a Democrat does take power (viz., Bill Clinton), we're quick to trash him. We don't like anybody in power, even if the powerful turn out to be ourselves.

So my advocacy of discipline might strike you as a hopeless exhortation. To hazard a generalization, lots of lefties could think of many things they'd rather do than go to meetings. Oscar Wilde, our scout from the late nineteenth century, is alleged to have said that the problem with socialism is that it would take too many evenings. (If he didn't say it, he should have.) And in his lifetime, popular culture didn't even have the pull and reach it has today—no Walkman, no MTV, no video games, no CDs or VCRs or DVDs, no Internet. Surely the triad of sex, drugs and rock 'n' roll does not comport well with political discipline. The we-want-it-all spirit of consumer fun—the dominant style in American culture—meshes poorly with the rigor required to work within political coalitions, promoting policies that fall short of the millennium, campaigning for candidates who will no sooner be elected than you will find yourself in disagreement with them. Win or lose, the politics of citizenship is rarely electrifying. Let's be honest and face our fear of boredom. Let's face the fact and overcome it—find ways to enliven our duties. Let's cultivate a love of the ordinary—Hoederer's virtue, and the Buddha's.

For politics is a human endeavor unlike many another. If you write a poem, you who sign your name at the bottom are wholly responsible. But politics—left, right, center, transcendent, whatever—requires deals and a blurring of authorship. You (in the singular) require you (in the plural), and you in the plural never speak with a single mind. This is why politics—all politics—is dangerous; unfortunately, it is also indispensable. If you secede from politics because you'd rather stay home and live a quieter, sweeter life or stick to your last or cultivate your garden, in effect you leave politics to the blindest, most unbalanced, meanest-spirited people. So if you want to make the world more tolerable, you really have no choice but to discipline yourself to collaborate with imperfect allies, not angels. I've been to lots of boring meetings, sat next to lots of folks who aren't my favorites, and I'm not done with either. So be it. I find my pleasures elsewhere.

Speaking of persistence, self-discipline, toleration, attendance at boring meetings and other practical virtues, forgive me another word about the Democratic Party and the Greens. At a time when Americans show such distaste for politics of any stripe whatsoever, Green energy is something to conjure with. But the limits of the presidential constitutional system are even more unyielding. To transform the winner-take-all electoral system into a European-style parliamentary system would require divine intervention. So like it or not, you either vote Democratic or you submit to rule by Republicans. The Democratic Party is the inescapable field where we win, lose or draw. Once again, the politics of responsibility confronts the politics of ultimate ends. If you green-wash yourself in the name of pure virtue, you get two things: first, the good feeling that comes from the pleasures of enlisting in the army of pure virtue, and second, Republican rule.

Yet the news is not as dreadful as you might fear. In most of the land, the Democratic Party is no impermeable fortress of corporate power. It's little more than an organizational shell and a fund-raising apparatus. Don't think of it as an ideological monster lorded over by a central committee but rather as a field of action—including your action, your leverage. As a Green, all your purity gets you is political marginality, with the added bonus—if you want to consider it a bonus—of demonstrated spoiler capacity. As a Green Democrat, you can win all the influence you could win from a third party, all the opportunity to make the case for your policies in primary campaigns and lobbying between campaigns, all the visibility (and more) you would get from a separate organization—and you might even learn something from having to confront the views of people who see the world differently. *There's* a challenge—to share the burdens and wonders of living amid your countrymen and -women, with all their heartening and unsatisfactory traits, their bad ideas alongside the good ones, their ordinariness. See why they believe what they believe without dismissing them as dupes hopelessly crippled by false consciousness. Then try winning them over.

Green rectitude is one case of a larger pitfall: self-enclosure. When you belong to a small minority—as I did in the sixties—on the one hand, it's a comfort to share your life with fellow believers: to read the same articles, get the same references, wince at the same insults, pass around the same jokes. Very much on the other hand, disbelievers are a drag. Why bother talking to them when there's so much they don't *get*? When you live in an echo chamber where your cheers boom and cheerleading substitutes for thought, you enclose yourself in a sect, though you may call it a movement. The world of the saved substitutes for the world as it is, full of the unsaved. So I appeal to you: Persevere, but don't bury yourself in an army of the right-minded. Beware the perilous rapture of shrinking your world to the tribe of the saved, the cheerleading good guys who brandish the same slogans, curse the same enemies, thrill to the same saints, whether their names are Che, Fidel, Ho, Malcolm, Huey, Noam, whomever.

All faith has its risks, and faith that guides action has more than most. You might as well embrace the paradoxical, inescapable dangers. Don't be ashamed to seek some power; be ashamed to renounce power, for those who seize the power you disown will leave you with your hapless scrupulousness and proceed to make the world worse. Renounce fanaticism and you're sure to be out-organized by less squeamish fanatics, but an excess of zeal will turn you into a monster if it doesn't burn you out first. If you look in the mirror and see Lenin staring back at you, giving advice on how to suppress unruly factions or preaching against music (Beethoven made him want to make nice to his enemies, said the founder of the Gulag), take a deep breath and back up. A bit of Buddhist detachment will serve you well. Dedicate yourself but don't be a tedious ascetic: If you suppress your fanciful side in the name of committed solemnity, somebody—possibly you—will pay. Think for yourself; think against yourself too. Are these enough paradoxes for one sitting?

8

▥ On Rendering unto Identity No More than Identity Is Due, or Limits of Comfort

Dear ——,

You may be thinking that paradoxes are all very well, but your most urgent imperative is something you don't feel paradoxical about: defending your identity. So a word on that explosive little category *identity*, as in *identity politics*, the insistence that the foundation of your political being is and ought to remain your race, ethnicity, religion, sexual preference, nationality or any other category you're born into or gravitate to.

We're all familiar with the identity line of thought, usually linked to groups defined by race, ethnicity, sex and sexual preference—the groups whose emergence is rooted in sixties movements. Like all clichés, it's easily parodied—and the worthy element is easily overlooked. But pressed too far, the preoccupation promotes hypersensitivity and condescension, inhibits intellectual lucidity, launches a thousand political correctness jokes (not many at the expense of straight white males), balkanizes the Left and leaves the Right claiming the mantle of universal values while defending plutocratic power and immense inequalities. Maybe identity politics is waning on campuses and maybe it isn't, but it still has the capacity to break up political coalitions such as the antisweatshop and environmentalist movements as activists fight over how many members of which ethnic groups are represented on their executive committees. So it's worth talking about.

Let's give identity politics its due. Your starting point is that your identity has been singled out for victimhood. You didn't choose it, but you refuse to walk away from it. People like you—people who look like you—are brutalized. You rightly note that whites, males, heterosexuals and so on have the luxury of deploring your identity fixations while refusing to acknowledge the privileges conferred by their own, well, identities. You're not in a mood to pretend away an egregious history. Who's demanding that anyway? Since when do top-dog identities have the right to cancel bottom-dog identities just because they cause them discomfort? So standing up for your identity amounts to liberating yourself. You not only think this, you feel it. Identity politics is a passion— which makes it hard to argue with, since an argument against your position (say, on affirmative action or reparations) feels like an attack on your being. You can't help but be wary of fairness buffs with much to gain from opposing special privileges for minorities.

Your passions are worthy, but be careful. To stand up against discrimination, you don't need identity politics. When you defend your rights, as you should, what you are really defending is social equality—and you do so most convincingly *as a citizen*, not as one of the persecuted. If you campaign against hate crimes, it's not because you think Muslims or Jews are superior, only that they have a right to go about their business. Since a Muslim can agree with a Christian, a Jew or an atheist about the right not to be murdered for blasphemy, say, democratic support has good prospects. Identity politics with its passionate claims may feel primordial but accomplishes less than you hope—and it stops thought. When identity prevails, how you think and what you want become functions of who you are, and your mission, as a political animal, is limited to getting to know your category and then figuring out what follows. Your identity is not only the position from which you see the world, it is something primordial—your root, foundation, culture, the basis of your learning, all presumed fundamental to who you are and what you think, mean and want. Your views, values, perspectives, even the definitions you hold to seem to derive from inheritances: thus what you say is and ought to be a reflex of your black femaleness, say, or white maleness. On this view, the goal of politics is to make sure your category is represented in power, and the proper critique of other people's politics is that they represent a category that is not yours.

Identity politics has enough roots to populate acres of offshoots. It thrives most especially on university campuses, where there is little or no practical impediment to the bureaucratization of ideas. Nourished there, outgrowths thrive—museums, publishers, bookstores, corporate diversity training, government regulations, uniform congressional districts. The postmodernist intellectual atmosphere institutionalizes the sense that cultural difference is fundamental. Today, identity politics has the allure that the grand narrative of Marxism once enjoyed. The preoccupation with identity seems on the surface more modest than the grand old daemon of total revolution, but equally it is a pathway to self-encapsulation. The cultivation of identity has been partly legitimized, partly denatured by the multiculturalist compromise that extends legitimacy to group identities to cool out actual or potential uproar from students, faculty and junior administrators.

Identity politics is not just produced by racism. Racism is always damnable, but it is not complacent to point out that powerful forces—of liberality and tolerance—are working against it, not least the drive toward freedom and autonomy in the human heart and mind. The history of racial oppression in the United States (as elsewhere) is dreadful, but racism has never been in such bad odor as it is today. Surely, then, the upsurge of identity politics must be explained by other factors. Surely, this is in no small part a response to uprootedness and identity confusion. Universalist attachments—patriotic, civic, ideological—have weakened. Once, forced acculturation ("Americanization") was mandatory for the children of immigrants; today, they grow up into segmented memberships. From discrimination and loss, they hope to distill something affirmative. So as uprootedness grows, so does the hunger for roots. Proclaiming a marginal identity is a salvage operation in the acid bath of modernity. By now, though, this is also a tradition, with a weight of its own. Odd, isn't it, to think of identity politics as a conservative move? Yet it is.

Here's another unacknowledged paradox: Identity politics courts certainty, but identity is fluid; it changes in time (the Irish race becomes the Irish ethnic group, and the descendants of people who identified themselves as Scotch-Irish prefer to identify themselves as Irish). Identity also changes in space (an African American visiting Africa becomes an American). Among the youth cultures of the great cosmopolitan cities today, identity swirls, dissolves, reformulates. Moreover, everyone exists in multiple, overlapping, sometimes conflicting categories: I'm a man, born during World War II, a Jew, an American, a New Yorker, heterosexual and so on. Who determines which of my identities matter, and by which criteria and under which circumstances is a difficult—actually, an undecidable—question. Actually, I in my freedom may choose among all the identity stamps or none of the above. In identity politics, however, there is pressure to choose sides and stay on the team.

Even when it takes on a radical temper, identity politics is interest-group politics. It aims to change the distribution of benefits, not the rules under which the distribution takes place. Interest-group politics has its uses—it can remedy symbolic slights such as the naming of football teams after Indians—but its limits cause cramping too. Minor irritations get confused with grand passions. Identity politics at its strongest strives to create coalitions, but bloc to bloc, not person to person. It tends to see everyone as a bloc representative. The past overwhelms the future. Pulling at scabs takes the place of political argument. Thinking your way toward political positions and practical strategies becomes secondary. In other words, identity politics partakes of the anti-intellectual mood. It mocks universalist hopes, refusing to feel inspired by the idea of "government of the people, by the people, for the people"—is such rhetoric not a rationalization imposed by dominant groups? When you hear renowned intellectuals insist that rights and wrongs belong to groups and do not bridge the divides of identity, no wonder you doubt that any reasoned position is possible.

Yet feelings of attachment, whatever their sources, are neither moral nor political arguments. During agonized nights of the soul, you may well wonder how in a democracy a minority can convert cohesion into victory. Most likely, it can't.

Fair's fair: The fact that *identity* is a buzzword doesn't make what it refers to worthless. Plenty of valuable terms acquire currency (if in degraded form), no fault of theirs. It's also true, crucial and worth repeating that proponents of identity politics did not all by themselves invent the categories in which some people place others to control and degrade them. Racism isn't the invention of people who shout "racism." The claim that we would be bathing blissfully in color blindness were it not for those irritating naysayers who insist on bringing up questions of unequal treatment by race at inconvenient moments is not only demonstrably false (look at statistics for infant mortality), it's an evasion. In the name of transcendent values we must resist this brand of cant along with the others.

Speaking of transcendent values, you have the right to be different—including the right to be different from the conventional ways of being different. You should insist on it, and you don't need any special credentials to do so. You don't need identity politics to condemn racial bigotry or hatred of gays. You can—you must—condemn them *as a human being*. To fight against torture practiced on the Haitian Abner Louima by Brooklyn police in 1997, and to insist on policies that would prevent such abuses, I need not be Haitian; and anyone who tells me that Louima is not his or her issue because that person is not in fact Haitian is not someone who takes human rights seriously. To fight against a Colorado referendum that would prevent cities from banning sexual discrimination against gays, I need not be gay; I must simply oppose turning gays into pariahs—that is, treating them as a minority whose rights ought not be protected. (Those who purport only to oppose "special rights for gays"—like those who opposed civil rights in the sixties—themselves claim a special right, namely, to oppress members of the minority they despise.) The maniac in Arizona who killed a Sikh, thinking him a Muslim, after September 11, 2001, and cried out, "I'm an American!" missed the main point about being an American—that it's an idea about a good way of life, not a nationality. You don't have to be Muslim to say so.

Identity overblown points backward—to an anchorage in the past. Yet politics has to point forward, not back, or we are lost. The point is not where you're coming from but where you—accompanied by your fellow travelers on earth—are going. Toward that end, of course, you need to take into account what people both like and unlike you are feeling. Identities may matter to people you want on your side. This is something you need to get a feel for. Listen to them. (Don't trust opinion polls: The question's precise wording matters enormously, and the respondents may not have thought the question mattered until the pollster asked.) Don't lose balance. And don't be smug about having transcended identity yourself. The past is not overcome so easily by acts of will, and modest amounts of identity politics may help deliver justice. Identity touches on raw spots, so defending your own identity—any of the partial identities that you choose—indeed engages passion. When stigmatized people defend their identities against slurs, the hurt is "only" symbolic, but symbols matter. So it's not wrong to resist slurs and discriminations. Alerting the populace adds to the general edification.

When politics collapses into identity, though, it suffers from the twin curses of disproportion and self-enclosure. The passions that arouse—the ones that make nerve endings tingle—also imprison. On American campuses (and not only there) since the sixties, it's easy, too easy, to fight for identity; oddly enough, it's too easy to win. Identity feels deep and concrete, while the economy, the environment and war feel remote, abstract. The rights with the strongest followings are rights that people claim insofar as they belong to victim groups. Conservatives, meanwhile, parade as defenders of everyone's freedom. American politics, with its interest-group pluralism, is peculiarly adept at channeling political energies toward distinct race- or group-specific measures.

Balkanization feels good, proper and natural to the groups concerned—and detracts from mobilizing for overarching goals. Identity groups may stand in the way of social equality—universal health care, stronger social solidarity, better education and collective goals of all sorts. While minorities are preoccupied with their distinct demands, they devote correspondingly less attention to mobilizing majorities in behalf of common needs. The common degenerates. So identity politics, however it makes the blood race, often enough glosses over a profound impotence.

Universities are marvelous and ought to be more so. (You might even consider campaigning for subsidized education, since odds are that you and your friends couldn't afford to stay in school without holding jobs.) Even under pressure, this is the time in your life when you're encouraged to be provoked, deepen your human experience, learn to think, cultivate your talents. Much can be said for politics on campus: they're communal, careless and frequently fun. The positive way to put it is that you've struck it rich in community. The less positive way is, the sandbox is comfortable. Rarely will campus authorities punish you for expressing your sense of grievance. You'll never again be so well protected. But fun is also a trap, and preoccupation with identity is an aspect of that trap.

Here's yet another reason to get off campus. Take some time off the college-graduate-school-professional-school track. It's not only good for your sense of reality, it's good for your politics. Spend summers and off time with union or environmental justice campaigns. Get to know people who don't spend their days monitoring petty slights or working out theoretical positions that theorists think they should be spending their time working out. Let the world shake you up—in other words, educate you.

9

On Anti-Semitism, the Socialism of Fools

Dear ——,

Usually, the worst to be said about the contemporary preoccupation with difference is that it wastes time and energy by distracting us from human commonality. But there's an ugly version of identity fever that's far worse than diversion—a raw bigotry that is morally egregious. I'm singling it out in this letter partly because it's disgusting, partly because it has a dire lineage, and partly because I am by birth one of the people at issue. You may feel that this phenomenon doesn't rate much attention. Of all the damnable facts of the world, why should I go to the trouble of condemning one in particular? For this reason: There is a special place in Hell for the crimes of your own side, for they not only inflict suffering and call into question the morality of your side, they also spread universal corruption. They confirm that politics is an immoral enterprise; they undermine the hope that justice can prevail and the world can improve. They break hearts, and faith.

There is a special infernal corner burning too for silence about the wrongs of your own side—specifically, the cover-ups that pepper the history of the Left. Putting your own flaws "in context" while refusing to do the same for the other side is a cheap way to smother criticism—one of the more slovenly evasions. Avoid like the plague the either-or thinking that demands your absolute allegiance and pins all the crimes on the other side. The longing for paradise on your own side turns into that very bad habit, suppression of truth in the name of loyalty. You can spend a lifetime perfecting such maneuvers. Or you may have to face another terrible consequence of cheerleading when the day arrives when you realize that your formerly impeccable worldview is flawed, and you are so shocked, distraught and bitter at having been misled that you turn your politics upside down and trade in one brand of apologetics for another. You don't want to become one of those born-again propagandists who makes a career out of claiming that everything he thought in the bad old days was utterly wrong, everything he thinks now is utterly right, and everyone who disagrees with either is dishonorable.

In the spring of 2002, a Palestinian student organization at San Francisco State University displayed a poster depicting a can of soup labeled with drops of blood, dead babies and the words CANNED PALESTINIAN CHILDREN MEAT, SLAUGHTERED ACCORDING TO JEWISH RITES UNDER AMERICAN LICENSE. Posters declared "Jews = Nazis." At one pro-Israel rally, a group of praying Jews, some of them survivors of the Nazi Holocaust, found themselves surrounded by a threatening crowd screaming, "Go back to Russia, Jew!" "Get out or we will kill you!" and "Hitler did not finish the job."

Reading an account of these events in horror but not, alas, complete amazement, I was reminded of the time during the Gulf War when a lunatic student at Berkeley, the head of an African-American splinter group, addressed a room full of antiwar faculty and students trying to overcome tensions within the movement. At an antiwar demonstration a few days earlier, I had heard this man shout out, "Read Henry Ford, *The International Jew!*"—a bilious screed that inspired Hitler. Now this man spat out venomously, "You Jews, I know your names, I know where you live," and the faculty in attendance, who would have erupted had this been a white student sneering at "you blacks," not "you Jews," sat stiffly and said nothing. Embarrassed? Frightened? Thinking it wasn't, well, *time* for this issue, it was off the agenda, an inconvenience?

The most that could be said for a response so restrained as to be indistinguishable from silence was that the outburst was too crazy to warrant a reply, that a reply would carry the burden of dignifying a lunatic accusation. This is how mindless drivel works, for to take time to refute racist nonsense and blatant threats can feel worse than distraction; you feel demeaned, hijacked, even to have to go to the trouble. Nihilistic speech works like bullying violence: by declaring that reason is beside the point, it undermines confidence that minds can ever meet. This is why you hear the strangest things on the farther shores of political lunacy, where the strangeness is not incidental to the kind of appeal these charges make. Indeed, it's central to the lunacy of fraudulent, racist charges that they be colossal fictions. During the Gulf War, a student declared to me that Arab Jew hatred doesn't qualify as anti-Semitism because Arabs are themselves Semites. By these loony lights, only anti-Arab sentiment qualifies as anti-Semitism. . . . Please note too how fixed obsessions of Jew hatred keep popping up, as if to mock any hope that reason might dispel them once and for all. The same idiocy about the impossibility of anti-Semitism cropped up at San Francisco State in 2002, and the web site of the Palestinian student group there included a link to the text of the Protocols of the Elders of Zion. During the Gulf War, a black student group at UCLA reprinted this same notorious forgery.

The tenacity of anti-Semitism is, to use an overused word precisely, awesome. To feel staggered by it, you shouldn't have to be Jewish. To feel revolted, you don't have to believe that Jews have a special title to suffering or that they are faultless or that the policies of a Jewish State are stamped with grace. Note too: Sharp criticism of Israeli policies is not what I mean by anti-Semitism here. Singling out Israel for special opprobrium—when more murderous regimes such as Sudan, Algeria and Russia fail to ignite comparable denunciation—gets closer, though not even this qualifies as raw anti-Semitism. Beholding a social wrong, the raw anti-Semite is quick to leap immediately upon "the Jews" with an eagerness that, if applied to any other group, would readily inspire the most vigorous condemnation. About rancid anti-Semitism there's nothing subtle.

In 1893, German socialist August Bebel called anti-Semitism "the socialism of fools," suggesting an embarrassing relation with the modern Left—embarrassing not because left-wing anti-Semitism is more pernicious than right-wing anti-Semitism, but because the Right believes in thinking with its blood while the Left is supposed to be rational. Jew hatred is probably the most durable of all racisms; certainly, it is the most promiscuous. Jew hating occupies an especially wide trough among the many bigotries, for across the centuries it has proved itself compatible with any number of ideological systems, having started as Christian (though in bad odor there currently), intermittently joined by many strands of Islam, and on and off coupled to the caricature of leftism in which capitalism is imagined to be a Jewish plot. Its respectability was high until the Nazi slaughterhouse gave it a bad name. In recent years, fueled by the Israeli Occupation, it swings up, down and sideways (though never to zero) in various guises—sometimes the crackpot gesture known as "Holocaust denial," sometimes more ferocious Nazi echoes. The arguments vary but the enemy is always familiar.

Anti-Semitism doesn't care about niceties. Like every other lunacy that diminished human brains are capable of, anti-Semitism doesn't need details. It always knows in advance what it hates. Israeli policies bring the ranters out of the woodwork, but their delusional rants and rank forgeries simmer beneath the surface, waiting for opportunity. The worst crackpot notions that circulate through the furious Middle East and its diaspora now roam America too—not least the demonstrably false claim that no Jews died in the Twin Towers on September 11 because they were phoned in advance (presumably in a conference call from the Elders of Zion) and told not to show up for work that morning. If this isn't bad enough, students themselves are spreading the gibberish. Students without intellectual standards—a deplorable phenomenon of our time, not unrelated to the preoccupation of many faculty with theoretical styles at the expense of logic.

You don't have to fear an Auschwitz repeat, a second Holocaust, to deplore the consequences. The dangers are palpable: In misguided solidarity with Palestinians, synagogues and other Jewish sites are attacked in Europe, North Africa and elsewhere. But history, for better or worse, is not a machine that repeats its moves. The graver danger is moral. A student movement is not just a student *movement* but a *student* movement. Regardless of politics, students have the responsibility of thinking and discerning—in short, studying. You know better, so don't stand idly by as the know-nothings ape the worst formulas of their elders. Whoever isn't revolted by anti-Semitic drivel should find time for soul-searching. If the unremitting fight against Jew hatred is not a "progressive" cause, then what kind of progress does the progressive side have in mind?

10

■ On Anti-Americanism, or the
Temptation of the Automatic *No*

Dear ——,

As I don't have to remind you, we find ourselves in wartime—or a warlike time—that is likely to stretch ahead without any obvious limit for two reasons. First, Islamist terrorists, apparently several thousand in number (but with expansive possibilities), have declared war upon the United States, by which they mean all its citizens. Massacres are righteous to them. Death is so fundamentally a means to their ends—to purify Islam, defeat infidels and establish their empire—that it becomes an end. Their membership is small but potentially elastic. Second, in the law of nations, self-defense is justified. But what the present government calls a War on Terrorism has no precise enemy and no precise terminus; it is over when and only when the government in power declares it over. We are called to war without end, against any force the White House declares to be our enemy.

So for the foreseeable future, much of what the government does at home (sorry, *homeland*) and abroad, and much of what we do as a people, will be defended as the necessary burden of war. Policies dangerous and unjust, along with the necessary and just, will be wrapped in *burkhas* of patriotic feeling. You may be accused of patriotic deficiency for intimating that George W. Bush was appointed president by a Republican majority in the Supreme Court, or that colossally greedy tycoons persuaded lawmakers to turn blind eyes (and upturned palms) to their immodest proposals, among them permission to melt polar icecaps with the warming effluents of SUVs from which their little American flags defiantly wave.

Whatever is to come, you and I need to think long and hard about how this is our war and how it is not. Skepticism is healthy; knee-jerking opposition isn't. Against the patriotism of cheerleading, we dare not sign onto every raid against liberty and every armed attack the authorities propose. But it is unconscionable—and self-defeating to boot—to say that security is someone else's problem, as it is wrong to declare unthinkingly that recourse to proportionate force cannot be just. The terrorists of September 11 were not the present-day reincarnations of Vietnamese Communists, who only hysterics thought were poised to climb ashore the beaches of San Diego. The Islamist murderers, though, did come ashore to annihilate as many American lives as feasible, heedless of the suffering they inflicted—or rather, reveling in that suffering, as proof of their righteousness—and they are committed to coming ashore again. Any movement that does not take seriously—not perfunctorily, not rhetorically but seriously—the need to protect Americans from murderous assaults of this magnitude does not deserve a hearing and will not get one.

Generals, it is said, are always planning to fight the last war—but they're not alone in suffering from sentimentality, blindness and mental laziness disguised as resolve. Antiwar movements are bound, against all the emotional comforts of repetition, to see the world freshly. A narrow-minded antiwar movement helps no one when it mires itself in its own mirror-image myths. Those who evade the difficulties in their purist positions and refuse to face *all* the mess and danger of reality only guarantee their bitter inconsequence. Moral and practical traps lie on every side. So let's pick our way carefully. We've lit out for new territory.

Here's the problem in a nutshell: In revulsion against the worst your government does, you'll be tempted to renounce your country. In revolt against the smug and bullying who praise America by telling you to shut up, you'll be tempted to skip the praise.

Refusing to praise the America that the authoritarians tell you to praise—just because it's they who have told you to do the praising—is infantile. (Eat your peas! *Nnnooo!*) The preordained *no* is a kind of submission. In the words of the American humorist Don Marquis, "An idea isn't responsible for the people who believe in it," and the same is true of a nation-state, even a powerful one, for people of many different opinions share membership in it. Disconcerting news for the purist; but the purist doesn't belong in politics. A purist who wishes to make the world better should design a beautiful object or leap into the stands to catch a fly ball or cook a sumptuous meal. Politics, a feat of collaboration, is something different. Without disconcerting bedfellows there is no politics—unless you are a totalist, in which case what you really want is the death of conflict, the death of difference—the death, really, of politics.

All that by way of prologue. Now, start by recognizing that your criticism is tied to your praise.

When you identify with your country—even against your will—and your country's actions offend your sense of decency, you suffer a blow to yourself: not to the "imagined community" (Benedict Anderson's phrase) that's called a nation but to your own visceral, moral being. This is like being betrayed by a lover. What you gave of yourself is now lost to yourself. The world reaches into you, grips your internal organs and squeezes. The outrage is also inrage. You burn to react. You're tempted to lash out in vengeance. You want more than to make life bearable, or just better; you want to recover your innocence.

Most of the sixties, and frequently since, I have groped for words to express, in the right proportions, the membership and the anger all at once. For me, the anger and the horror started when I launched into activism as a campaigner against American nuclear weapons policy in 1960, and then on through the Bay of Pigs invasion of Cuba, American collusion in South African apartheid and most of all, the egregious war in Vietnam. But for some reason one particular moment in March 1965 stands out. I was twenty-two, living among the SDS circle in Ann Arbor, Michigan, helping to organize the first national demonstration against the Vietnam War. The war was already a daily assault on brains and conscience, and so I could scarcely bear to watch the TV news. But one evening I turned on the NBC News for some reason and saw U.S. Marines occupying Santo Domingo while young Dominicans protested. On the scale of enormities, it was only a tiny exercise in old-fashioned imperialism, this expedition into the Caribbean to keep a military junta in power and block the restoration of an elected social-democratic govern-ment. I don't know why these particular pictures of young Dominicans resisting the Americans stirred me so deeply. I don't know what I felt more keenly: horrified disbelief that my country could be waving the wrong flag, betraying its better self, or horrified belief that my country could only be doing something so appalling be-cause *it*—not its policies, not this or that wretched deci-sion, but *it* in the core of its dark heart—was committed to suppressing the rights of inconvenient peoples. Gun-boat diplomacy, we learned to call this, in my high school history class. How do you reform a leviathan?

I remember writing a poem that night—not a good one, but a sincere one. I was a nonviolent twenty-two-year-old and I wanted to stand with the young anti-Americans in the Dominican Republic: The poem ended with a romantic line about "a rifle and a sad song." An-other phrase I like better sticks out in my memory: *I would only curse America, like a drunkard his bottle*. Amer-ica, love it and leave it at once.

You can fall in love with your outrage. I have felt such moments of horrified recognition countless times since, and devoted many waking hours to fighting against an appalling American foreign policy obsessed with communism, oil and easy access to markets at the cost of human rights. In the second half of the sixties and early seventies, it felt to me that I was choking on the Vietnam War, that the fight against the war had become my life. The war went on so long and so destructively, it felt like more than the consequence of a wrongheaded policy—I felt that my country was revealing some fundamental core of wrongness by going on and on with an indefensible war. The American flag did not feel like my flag, even though I could recognize—in the abstract—that it made sense for others to wave it in the antiwar cause, and I argued against waving the North Vietnamese flag or burning the Stars and Stripes. The flag did not feel any more congenial to me in the early seventies as the Nixon administration widened the Vietnam War into Laos and Cambodia and connived in the Pinochet coup, or in the eighties as Reagan endorsed the Nicaraguan Contras, the Salvadoran and Guatemalan death squads. To put it mildly, my generation of the New Left relinquished any title to patriotism without terribly much sense of loss because the perpetrators of unjust war had run off with the *patrium*. The nation had congealed into an empire, whose logic is unwarranted power.

Read history with an open eye and it is hard not to notice an American empire. On grounds of justice, you have to oppose it. Honest conservatives acknowledge imperial power too—though enthusiastically, without limits. What is Manifest Destiny, the onward march westward, if not a robust defense of *righteous* empire? What was S. I. Hayakawa's brag about the Panama Canal, "We stole it fair and square," if not a sly recognition of the truth? You need not subscribe to the Left's grandest claims that America from its birth is—*essentially*—genocidal and indebted to slavery for much of its prosperity to acknowledge that white colonists took the land, traded in slaves and profited immensely thereby; or that the United States later lorded it over Latin America (and other long-time properties such as the Philippines), to guarantee cheap resources and otherwise line American pockets. If all this lording over does not rise to the level of colonialism in the strict sense (land grabs, political takeovers), and if it can be acknowledged that empires may have benign consequences (especially when they are displacing worse empires)—even for far-flung peoples far from the metropolitan core—then still, American wealth, resource access, military power and unilateralism qualify as imperial reach. Add that America, counting some 4 percent of world population, uses about one-quarter of the world's nonrenewable, environment-wrecking fossil fuel energy—and the administration of George W. Bush proposes to keep doing so as long as it likes, while the icecaps melt.

Still, what America learned on September 11 is that we do not monopolize destructive power. There are connoisseurs of apocalypse in the world, forces such as al-Qaeda that are more than willing to slaughter Americans (not to mention inconvenient others) in the name of their own version of empire. Indisputably, there are forces in the world that, if victorious, would leave the world far worse off than American power. For examples, you don't have to look any further than the Nazi and Japanese empires, or the Islamist rule that al-Qaeda longs for (insofar as it troubles to offer any "decent respect to the opinions of mankind" and "declare the causes which impelled them" to their massacres).

Yet there are those on the Left who on principle pooh-pooh the danger of a fanatical Islamist sect that sets no limits to what and whom it would destroy. Whoever is killed in America, Americans must still end up the greatest of Satans. Thus did Noam Chomsky go out of his way to belittle the September 11 attacks—so incredibly far as to claim, in a Belgrade radio interview as the ash still rained on lower Manhattan, that the U.S. was responsible for vastly more deaths in Sudan after the mistaken bombing of a pharmaceutical plant in 1998. All this on the strength of the thinnest of evidence. Intent on blaming America first, these anti-Americans will bend and select the reports and rumors that suit them to find respectable reasons for anti-American sentiment, which they always regard as derivative—not exactly blameless, but surely more than a bit justifiable. From the legitimate fear that misguided American policy has the effect of recruiting more terrorists, the harder anti-Americans leap to the unwarranted assumptions that terrorists are not terrorists or are only the most minor of terrorists, and thus do not have to be stopped.

Now, you and I are all too familiar with these temptations. We are intimate with the emotions of rejection. We dispute American policies too—and we do not shrink from the task. This is why you and I are obliged to educate Americans in the ways of the world, including the reasonable and unreasonable reasons why American policies are sometimes hated. We know that if the murderers despise American foreign policy, Americans need to reckon with this hatred—not because the hatred is automatically warranted, but because we find it wise not to inspire, not to provide rationalizations for, more crimes. But don't confuse your educational duty with the lazy assumption that the haters are right because we are powerful. In some university precincts, when you say *empire*, *power*, *colonial*, *dominant*, *hegemonic*, behold! A bolt of lightning flashes with a crash of cymbals, and the words are supposed to settle the question of what to think or do—oppose them! Why should it be so hard to grasp the obvious truth that there are worse fates than American power? Two decades of shallow academic obsession with the ugliness of power leave the Noam Chomsky–Gore Vidal Left (which is the only Left visible in many places) intellectually disarmed to entertain the possibility that power can be power for the good as well as for the bad, that it is frequently both, and that some sorts of power are worse—far worse, unspeakably much worse—than others.

Far better to acknowledge and wrestle with the strange and perverse dualities of America: the liberty and arrogance twinned, the bullying and tolerance, myopia and energy, standardization and variety, ignorance and inventiveness, the awful heart of darkness and the self-reforming zeal.

Indisputably, America ranks at the top of powerful nations. With the government at its service, American capital rewards dependents when it chooses, wreaks havoc when it chooses, proclaims an indiscriminate right to war, and places much of the world ecology at risk. So the words *American imperialism* are not so crazy after all to an American of New Left vintage gripped by radical disappointment, having learned in his teens that the CIA-backed coups in Iran (1953) and Guatemala (1954) caused unrelenting suffering, and who went on to watch with horror as the U.S. sidled up to (or worse, instigated) brutal dictatorships in Nicaragua, the Congo, Brazil and Chile, to name only a few. Issue after issue of *I. F. Stone's Weekly*, *The Nation* and the old *New Republic* and books by serious reporters such as David Wise and Thomas Ross brought fresh evidence that the U.S. sided with tyrannies and sought not only containment but markets and cheap resources. To see the American politics of the cold war as an extension of traditional gunboat diplomacy and corporate grabs wasn't hard.

The Left peered through American ideals and discovered behind them the hard material facts of money interest and blatant power. It wasn't hard to tear through freedom-loving rhetoric to spot America's raw and frequently callous self-interest, which had less to do with the freedom of downtrodden populations than with the freedom of the United Fruit Company to keep its labor costs down. Even the highest-minded of cold war ideals—containment of Communist military power—was tainted by the post-Hiroshima nuclear menace, and the spirit of "Better Dead than Red" refused to reckon with what was monstrous in the deployment of weapons of mass destruction.

Communism was a gift to the legitimacy of American power, but Vietnam's shooting war, with casualties in the millions, discredited the assumption of automatic righteousness once and for all. The doomed, reckless atrocities of the Vietnam War convinced a majority of Americans that poisonous communism—an "evil empire" if ever there was one—was not wisely or morally or successfully fought by napalm against a popular nationalist movement. The popular struggle against the Vietnam War—the most successful antiwar movement in history—changed America not only for the better but for good. Skepticism was vindicated—more than vindicated. The assumption of automatic American virtue was knocked reeling. One could now *assume* that the White House lied, that the CIA had contempt for democracy, that American interests were more self-seeking and less freedom loving than cold war rhetoric proclaimed.

Yet American policy since the sixties—heavily *because of* the sixties—is not so easily dismissed. Jimmy Carter's human rights concerns, easily mocked and inconsistently pursued, revealed an America more complicated than the cartoonish charge of "Yankee imperialism" implied. In Afghanistan, notably, and with unpleasant consequences, the U.S. boosted Islamic fundamentalism over secular communism. While in the eighties Ronald Reagan reconstructed the idea of a virtue monopoly under cover of a revived cold war, George H. W. Bush found in the Gulf War to free Kuwait from Baghdad's conquest a cause that the U.N. Security Council could embrace. Too slowly, in Bosnia, then in Kosovo, Bill Clinton revived the tradition of liberal interventionism—along the way, whatever the hard Left may think, putting the lie to the claim that the U.S. is always hell-bent on punishing Islam. In Bosnia and Kosovo, the war was in behalf of Muslims. (In Muslim-free Rwanda, the U.S., the U.N. and the rest of the world's powers shamefully failed to act.)

After the Clinton interlude, today's Republican unilateralism—rejection of the Kyoto atmospheric agreement, rejection of the international criminal court, rejection of the small arms and biological weapons treaties, abrogation of the antiballistic missile treaty and so on—represents a terrible throwback. After September 11, the fanatical cowboy elite in Washington squandered a great deal of goodwill. They cannot begin to understand why America's inordinate wealth and dominion might be dangerous. These are limited people, shaped by corporate (especially oil) backgrounds, convinced of their manifest destiny to bend the world to their liking. Men (and a few women) from the center and south of the country share its volatile mixture of insularity and swashbuckling, its suspicion of foreigners, its presumption of uncomplicated moral virtue. Like many of their countrymen and -women, they are, as essayist Anne Taylor Fleming put it, serial innocents, ever bruised, ever restored, ever fantastical in their ambitions. Their sentimentality about American goodness is bottomless. Their expectation that allies should cheerfully follow along is amazingly smug. It's a bit late in the game to excuse American support of atrocious regimes with a reminder that we fought fascism. That Europe should forget its gratitude is not surprising—but the day World War II ended was closer to 1900 than to the day you read these words.

You're right to burn with indignation about the policies streaming out of Washington. I do. But as you oppose thoughtless, jingoistic, cruel policies—and you must—please don't discredit yourselves by reviving the left-wing fundamentalism that erupted here and there on the Left in the wake of September 11, when anger at American policies slid easily into a negative faith in America the Ugly—what was taken to be the essential America, with its military bases, powerhouse investors and raucous culture. As the infernal smoke from the Twin Towers poured down on Manhattan, we heard from compassionate foreigners expressions of hope that September 11's crimes against humanity might elicit from Americans a stronger feeling for the whole of assaulted humanity. Memorably, writing in several European newspapers, the Chilean Ariel Dorfman recalled another September 11, this one in 1973, the day of the American-supported coup that overthrew the elected Allende regime and installed a bloody dictatorship. Dorfman wrote, "One of the ways for Americans to overcome their trauma and survive the fear and continue to live and thrive in the midst of the insecurity which has suddenly swallowed them is to admit that their suffering is neither unique nor exclusive, that they are connected—as long as they are willing to look at themselves in the vast mirror of our common humanity—with so many other human beings who, in faraway zones, have suffered similar situations of unanticipated and often protracted injury and fury."

Dorfman wrote compassionately. I think of his words again when I see a photo of Bosnian Muslims, marking the sixth anniversary of the Srbrenica massacre (7,000 to 9,000 dead at the hands of Serbian soldiers), *praying for the Americans who died September 11*—and wonder when American survivors of September 11 will set aside time to remember the victims of slaughter overseas. But you will recall (I certainly do) other critics returning to the rancid formula that the "real question" was *America's* victims—as if there could not be room in the heart for more than one set of victims. On campuses, in the list-servs of the Left, you (like me) heard a loud, dull clangor of anti-American reflexes and tones—smugness, acri-mony, Schadenfreude, the sense that the September 11 attacks were, well, not just desserts, exactly, but . . . damnable yet understandable payback . . . our responsi-bility, really (put it mildly), or fault (less mildly) . . . blowback from rotten American policies . . . rooted in America's own crimes of commission and omission . . . reaping what empire had sown. Was not America essen-tially the oil-greedy, Islam-disrespecting oppressor of Iraq, Sudan, Palestine? Were not the ghosts of the Shah's Iran, of Vietnam and the cold war Afghan *jihad* rattling their bones?

The anti-American didn't want simply to change American *policies*—in Iraq, in Israel-Palestine, in Saudi Arabia, to name three, all eminently worth changing. The anti-American burned with zeal to confirm the wickedness of the United States at its core. In the car-toon view that emerges most incessantly from Noam Chomsky, nothing anywhere is worse than American power—not the women-enslaving Taliban, not the unre-pentant al-Qaeda committed to kill Americans anywhere just as they please. No, America is nothing but a self-seeking bully, the worst terrorist state in the world. America's essence is frozen: It values only raw force and untrammeled capital. It does not face genuine dilemmas. It never has legitimate reason to do what it does. When its rulers' views command popularity, this can only be because the entire population has been brainwashed or rendered moronic or shares in the monstrous values of the ruling class.

Like jingoists who consider it immoral to make an effort to understand terrorists—they prefer to shoot first—the bitter-end anti-American thinks nothing is complicated about America and its works. From a practical viewpoint, their caricature dooms them to defeat, for logically, if America is as uniformly brutal and closed as they believe, there can be no regeneration. America is finished—there is nothing to do but preach at the funeral. But the anti-American is not practical. His prime rhetorical goal is to inflame, thus to confirm that he is marginal and therefore virtuous. Nor is he curious, for he knows the answer to all questions before he asks them. He claims that to "contextualize" the actions of various mass murderers is important (for example, the Khmer Rouge and al-Qaeda) but refuses to consider any but the least flattering context for American policy. Before condemning a whole nation that has reason to fear more massacres, ought we not trouble ourselves to understand America, this freedom-loving, brutal, tolerant, shortsighted, selfish, generous, trigger-happy, dumb, glorious, fat-headed, heartbroken and frightened powerhouse?

Not a bad place to start might be the patriotic fervor that arose after the attacks. Here's a brief anatomy of my own anti-anti-Americanism—a surprise to me, by the way (but in a stricken world, we should not be afraid to be surprised). By hanging a flag from our balcony a mile from the site of the World Trade Center, my wife and I did not mean to join a stampede. We wanted to affirm—

to affirm plainly—solidarity with the lost and with the heroic rescuers, to declare that we belonged to a people and that our fate was bound up with theirs. After disaster we felt the desire to reassemble the shards of a broken community, to withstand the loss, to avert worse. The attack stirred in us some ordinary feelings: love of our people, pride in their endurance and the desire to keep them from being hurt anymore. As is normal in the course of human events, we inverted the wound and transformed it into protest ("we didn't deserve this"), indignation ("they can't do this to us") and resolve ("they won't defeat us"). Pride is many-pronged: It can fuel the quest for justice, the rage for punishment or the pleasures of smugness. The dangers are obvious. Yet it should not be hard to understand that for many of us in the days after September 11, the American flag became a badge of belonging, not a call to shed innocent blood.

In the absolute anti-Americanism of al-Qaeda, because the United States maintains bases in the land of the Prophet, innocents must be slaughtered and their temples crushed. Totalitarians such as Osama bin Laden treat issues as fodder for the apocalyptic imagination. They want absolute power and call it God. Were Saddam Hussein or Hamas to win all their demands, al-Qaeda would move on, in their next video, to another issue—for the issue is not the issue, power is. The murderers of September 11 did not trouble themselves with any nice distinctions. Osama bin Laden himself declared to the world in a video after September 11, "America has been filled with horror from north to south and east to west, and thanks be to God. . . . God has blessed a group of vanguard Muslims, the forefront of Islam, to destroy

America. May God bless them." The murderers did not, like the Vietnamese of the sixties and seventies, distinguish between the American government and the American people. They slammed into towers that were at once cathedrals of American might and buildings full of human beings. They were not interested in the possibility that some of their victims descended from civil rights workers and others from the Ku Klux Klan, some were Mexican busboys and others, Muslims. They did not canvass 354 firefighters for their views of American bases in Saudi Arabia. Had they known that one young man, Mark Bingham, who apparently helped bring down the second hijacked jet headed for Washington, was gay, they probably would have agreed with Jerry Falwell and Pat Robertson that he was one of the infidels who proved America ripe for destruction. No fault of theirs that they killed "only" some 3,100 people—many of them not Americans, by the way—and not the 50,000 estimated to work in the World Trade Center on a normal day. Could it be plainer that these attacks were terror not only against the American state but also against the American people? To name these attacks "War on America" was not media hype.

By contrast, soft anti-Americans don't condone mass slaughter. Grant them that they sincerely want U.S. policies to change—though by their lights, such turnabouts are well nigh unimaginable. Terrorism, the multiplication of death and fear, is just not the heart of the matter, which for them is American crime past, present and future. Americans are "the real terrorists"—always (and by implication al-Qaeda consists of unreal terrorists, minor diversions). Whatever happens, one wheels automatically to blame America first. The mass murderer—if not the mass murder—was "manufactured" by the U.S. itself. One not only notes but gloats that the U.S. built up Islamic fundamentalism in Afghanistan as a counterfoil to the Russians. Causation (which is exaggerated, but never mind) becomes destiny. Al-Qaeda is an effect, not a cause, a symptom, not a disease. The initiative, the power was and must always remain American. A symptom cannot be held accountable. To the left-wing fundamentalist mind, the only interesting or important brutality is at least indirectly the United States' doing. This applies to the future as well: Thus one automatically disapproves of war against the Taliban-Qaeda alliance, preferring action to bring them to justice—as if a criminal justice system were in place to issue warrants against Osama bin Laden, to parachute marshals into the fastness of Afghanistan to arrest him, try him and punish him.

Please reject these evasions. Avoid mental laziness. Oppose Washington's wrongheaded policies—the clique in charge will want to extend the War on Terrorism far and wide to whatever Axis of Evil catches their animosity—but don't let your opposition blind you to dangers that the reigning powers did not imagine: real terror networks that aim to command real weapons of mass destruction. Faced with the uniquely murderous challenge of al-Qaeda, don't think you are looking at napalm in Vietnam or Guatemalan peasants seeking higher pay in the coffee fields. If the U.S. pursued bad policies in the past, as it did, what follows? Having bolstered fundamentalist Islamism in Afghanistan two decades ago in an anti-Soviet cause, is the United States condemned to helpless blowback forever? Doesn't a bad history require of us a responsibility to rectify the damage? By such a line of reasoning, since some American companies and rightists welcomed Hitler, America should never have fought Nazi Germany. Since the U.S. tilted toward Iraq against Iran during the awful war of the eighties, the Iraqi invasion of Kuwait in 1990 should have been welcomed. Since Saddam Hussein slaughtered tens of thousands of Kurds with chemical weapons in 1988 and the U.S. looked on uncomplainingly, the U.S. once and for all forfeited the moral right to oppose his weapons of mass destruction.

In the name of freedom and reason, do not succumb to the false and disingenuous claim that if the U.S. once (or twice or a hundred times) did wrong, it cannot now do right and is not obliged to do so. Don't sink into the assumption that the U.S. is a smoothly rounded, unified metaphysical entity. Face up to America's self-contradictions, its on-again off-again interest in extending rights, its clumsy egalitarianism coupled with ignorant arrogance. Argue about policies but discard the anti-American prejudice that musters evidence to suit a prefabricated conclusion. Insofar as we who criticize U.S. policy want Americans to wake up to the world, we must speak *to*, not *at*, Americans, in recognition of our common perplexity and vulnerability. We must listen to them, force ourselves to hear what makes us uncomfortable, abstain from the fairy-tale pleasures of oversimplification and overcome the overbearing assumption that we already know all we need to know. We must not content ourselves with hearing what Washington says and rejecting that. We must forego the luxury of disdain and be citizens—which does not mean we turn our backs on those who are not, but that we take our fellow citizens seriously and imagine ourselves responsible for them, as we would want them to be for us.

Terrorists remind us, you and I, that we share the common condition of citizens, that we are subject to all they are subjected to, that we cannot secede.

11

On Patriotism Without Embarrassment, or Saving the World Again

Dear ———,

If we forego the luxury of disdain, it is not to embrace the patriotism of silence.

In the mid seventies, a student of mine at the University of California, Santa Cruz, used to drive a VW van with a bumper sticker that read QUESTION AUTHORITY. She was an antinuclear activist, though her van didn't say so. One day, somebody scratched out the slogan. I think of her and the anonymous vandal in this time of strident certitudes and unasked or barely asked questions, when many authorities think loyalty is to be demonstrated with a shut mouth.

Whoever exacted vengeance for that young woman's audacity was stomping on democratic ideals, failing to understand that questioning is precisely what authority *needs*. Only in an autocracy is doubt a breach of decorum. The ruler is absolute and infallible—end of discussion. In a democracy, however, authority needs to be convincing. It cannot be convincing, cannot care for the public good, unless pressed to defend itself. This is what John Stuart Mill meant in *On Liberty* when he wrote that even if one and only one person dissented, the dissent should be heard, for two reasons. First, the dissenter might always be right. Second, the authority of the majority opinion—even if close to unanimous—is heightened by having to confront its contraries. In the light of free competition, arguments only improve. So the expression of rival views is necessary for practical as well as principled reasons.

Since September 11, 2001, we hear the thunder of stampedes all around. Ari Fleischer, the president's press secretary, scolded that people should "watch what they say." He was not referring to advance notice of troop movements, but a tossed-off remark by a talk show host. Attorney General Ashcroft admonished, "To those who pit Americans against immigrants, citizens against noncitizens, to those who scare peace-loving people with phantoms of lost liberty, my message is this: Your tactics only aid terrorists for they erode our national unity and diminish our resolve." Such unreasoning lack of faith was echoed by others who should have known better. Journalist Gregg Easterbrook wrote in the *Wall Street Journal* that, since novelists Barbara Kingsolver and Arundhati Roy had written harshly about the American flag and the American approach to the world, "bookstores may fairly respond by declining to stock" their books. Stocking their books, in his view, amounted to "promoting" their views.

As it happens, I had criticized some of Roy's views, along the lines of my previous letter, and vigorously disagreed with Kingsolver about the flag. So? What does their wrongheadedness have to do with their right to be read? As it happens, Easterbrook himself had just written in *The New Republic* that American motorists contributed handsomely via oil imports to the Saudi Arabian money gusher that subsidized al-Qaeda. Should gasguzzling patrons of Barnes and Noble be catered to if they demand that his own book be unshelved? A kind of madness is streaming across America. I'm guessing that it isn't the last time we smell hysteria in the air.

Resist this mind-shuttering panic. Policy unquestioned is policy unbridled. If our authorities are already unthinkingly, knee-jerkingly disbelieved by too many people around the world, no one helps anything by asking them fewer questions. Don't let politicians off the hook when they shut themselves up, as the loyal but feeble opposition is prone to do. Their timorousness dovetails with the authorities' pathetic lack of confidence in their own arguments. That the quandaries we confront now—and for the foreseeable future—are immensely difficult surely makes the asking of questions a citizen's duty. A patriotic gag rule is the opposite of useful.

Patriotism should not be confused with obedience. *Obedience* is obedience. There are some good times for it—heeding the fire marshals in a crowded theater. Yet the fact that obedience can be passed off as patriotism suggests the poor condition of actual patriotism—useful affirmations of solidarity, not feeble symbolic gestures.

Patriotism is not scapegoating but love—love of one's people, love of their ideals, and not just idle belief but steady action. In America, this rare nation whose highest identity is formed from allegiance to ideas and not ancestral blood, patriotism is love of constitutional principle. Alas for the malefactors of simplification, our traditions are multiple, and you should do what you can do to see that everyone sees all the traditions, sees them whole. Surely the World War I tradition of jailing opponents, firing them from universities, shutting down newspapers, blocking their mailing privileges, is a dubious contribution to the patriotic weal. Surely the World War II tradition of rounding up Japanese-Americans deserves the denunciation, recompense and apology that it much belatedly occasioned. Surely the fight against the original, authentic axis of evil would have benefited from some persnickety debate over the justice of these policies in wartime universities.

The patriotic gag rule is a tradition too, though not one to be proud of. But in today's patriotic silence there sounds a particular strain and fear. The political closure, the meager debates, the harshness occasionally on display against dissidents and immigrants betray a shortage of genuinely patriotic activity. We do not lack for ceremonies—televised, preferably. We display lapel pins and antenna flags galore. But we lack for patriotism on the ground, patriotism lived. The displays are easy and empty. Fights over school curricula brim with cheap intensity. Yet serious patriotism entails readiness to sacrifice. In George W. Bush's America, there is talk of volunteering, of service, and there are recruitment campaigns, but what rings louder is the clangor of material acquisition. Profiteering is normal. (Another tradition.) Despite the recent Wall Street scandals, government policies still reward the top tycoons, and there are few signs that rock-bottom reform is in the cards. With government encouragement, corporations rush offshore to circumvent taxes. They avail themselves of tax provisions written for them by supine politicians. Few of the wealthy lift a finger to relinquish their privileges unless compelled to do so. We are at war without a draft, without rationing, without air-raid wardens, without the public service of dollar-a-year men. (Imagine, in today's climate, dollar-a-year CEO's willing to sacrifice their annual multimillions!)

Readiness to sacrifice entails not just wearing flag lapel pins or wishing American troops well, but willingly sacrificing privilege in the name of the greater good. We should recall that when skyscrapers were on fire, we needed firefighters and police officers, not Enron hustlers or Arthur Andersen accountants. We should be questioning whether it is a supreme act of patriotism to boost subsidies for corporate farmers, expedite moving electronic corporate headquarters offshore to tax havens and swell the riches of billionaires when the ratio of CEO income to average worker income in top companies is of the order of 500 to 1. (In 1973, it was 45 to 1.) Real patriots should scorn an administration that passes out capital gains and inheritance tax relief to the plutocracy, who risk nothing, whatever the fortunes and misfortunes of their companies, and whose idea of sacrifice is that somebody in a blue collar should perform it for low wages. We should be questioning whether the most complete expression of citizenship and patriotic duty is to head for the mall or Disney World, as George W. Bush advised after September 11. We should be doubting that America is rightly at war with whomever the president says we are, just when he says so.

And we should be indignant about the immense failures of intelligence that afflicted American institutions before September 11—and I do not refer simply to the feebleness and pettiness of the FBI, CIA and other government agencies. I refer to the collective dismissal of intelligence in a culture of gluttony, glibness, mediocrity and evasion—gluttony for those who can afford it, though not only them; glibness, mediocrity and evasion for everyone. I refer to the insularity, shallowness, propagandistic bombast, the collective and individual narcissism of American media drowning the public in sleek entertainment and chatter, failing to connect dots of news into comprehensible patterns. I take as a tiny symbolic victory for stupidity the notion that extensive travel around the world and even (perish the thought!) knowledge of the names of foreign leaders is held somehow to be a disqualification for leadership of the United States, and that ignorance is, while not perhaps the most admirable of traits, considered an ingratiating quality in a commander in chief.

So I want to put in a good word for patriotism but insist that what patriotism needs most is not a pat on our collective back, not self-congratulation or catechisms, but rather intelligent skepticism, including a higher skepticism about patriotism, and a willingness to sacrifice. Patriotism needs action. Programs will depend on the moment but some principles are essential. Liberal patriotism is not quick to war but it recognizes this necessary paradox of a globalized world: To make the world safer for Americans, we need to make it safer for more than Americans. Against oil-based myopia, patriots ought to clamor to phase out the oil dependency that overheats the earth and binds us to tyrants.

Surely many Americans are primed for a patriotism of action, not pledges. What better time to crack the jingoists' claim to a monopoly of patriotic virtue? Instead of letting minions of corporate power run away with the flag, we need to remake the tools of our public life—our schools, social services, transport. We need national service—not just an option but a mandate. We need to remember that the exemplary patriots are the members of the emergency community of mutual aid who brought down Flight 93, not the born-again war devotees who cherish martial virtues yet somehow succeeded in getting themselves deferred from the armed forces.

We have an opening now, freed of our '60s flag anxiety and our automatic *No*. It's time for a liberal patriotism, robust, unapologetic and uncowed. It's time for pride in democracy, not slavishness. It's time for the patriotism of mutual aid, not symbolic displays. It's time to diminish the gap between the nation we love and the justice we also love. It's time for the real America to stand up.

But without you, dear activist, none of this will happen.

If I haven't already heaped up too many tasks, let me conclude with a mountainous one. Thinking about what to do now requires lifting our hearts and minds into a time frame as uncomfortable as it is uncustomary—extracting ourselves from an itchy, onrushing culture, where the new and hot are perpetually demolishing the old and the not hot. We need to climb onto another plane.

Humans are the animals who know that we die. This poses a problem, to put it mildly, because we are automatically afflicted—or gifted—with knowing there's a difference between our corporeal condition and our future. Simply put, we think beyond our bodies. We anticipate. We experience presence but know (at some level) that a future is on its way from which we will be absent. This discrepancy is the source of much human civilization. It is certainly the origin of religions, which are ways to imagine something that transcends the fate of our own bodies. But also buildings, governments, institutions and creations of all sorts express our desire to throw lifelines into the future, to make sense of our finitude.

This is the background against which I understand two huge contemporary facts: weapons of mass destruction, and the ongoing human destruction of the world, especially the remaking of global climate—an enormity we try to keep at bay with the clinical words *the environment*, as if it were a thing that stood safely outside ourselves. Weapons and reckless machines rework the ancient, fundamental human predicament on a scale never before in play. They transpose mortality from the level of the individual human being to the level of humanity. They change human nature because they make human beings conditional. In the nuclear age, humans are born as hostages. With the spread of the knowledge to build weapons of mass destruction comes the proliferation of the power of the executioner, as Robert Jay

Lifton has said. Face to face with executioners, and with our own inertia, the human species becomes dimly aware it must fight for the right to live.

It seems to me not so surprising that we—even activists—resist coming to grips with this new human condition. It requires of us an unprecedented response. Our imagination is taxed. The problems are urgent but do not feel like emergencies. Life goes on, and for the fortunate ones, it's rather good. The dangers stretch far beyond the dangers we feel today or those we anticipate in our lifetimes, and they are freshly upon us, for we're only in the second half century of the nuclear age and have only begun to recognize that the habitability of the earth cannot be taken for granted. For the rest of our lives, we will wonder, and wonder again, what to do—what action is commensurate with the need.

Perhaps—who knows?—we might surprise ourselves. We might even stand at the edge of an auspicious turn in world history. The ideas of the Enlightenment, which were the founding ideas of the American Republic two centuries ago, conceived of human beings as possessed of rights by virtue of being born human. We were not bound to the circumstances of our birth, and we were not to be subjected to the will of arbitrary authority. As humans, we were said to be in possession of inalienable rights. But the Enlightenment thinkers in their various ways understood that we were also in need of governments to exercise power over human beings. How to turn this neat trick—the limitation of rights in the name of rights? The American founders had a constructive idea: secure life, liberty and the pursuit of happiness through a democratic republic.

Now, in an age when humanity's powers are vastly multiplied, the problem is how to secure another human right: freedom from the fear of extermination. Strangely enough, there are reasons for hope. "In a dark time, the eye begins to see," as Theodore Roethke wrote. Collectively, fitfully, the world has begun to develop sensibilities that are genuinely global. Human rights, interdependence, sustainable development—these watchwords have become clichés because the principles and claims are inescapable. The American government may reject them, but there are international courts. There are international police powers, embryonic, crippled, lethargic, but their principles are in play. I'm not complacent about how far we've come toward securing a human future, yet the growth of institutions such as the Hague human rights court tells me that we might be on our way, if not toward a federal world government, then at least toward a sort of Articles of Confederation in which we collectively agree that the enforcement of the collective good trumps the national boundaries that were the great political achievement of the eighteenth and nineteenth centuries.

There are reasons for hope but never guarantees. We, my generation, weren't the first to make mistakes. You won't be the last. Above all, there are reasons to act, and a strong probability that if the wise do not act wisely, the fools will prevail—and anyway, since when does hope require reasons? If we're strong, wise and lucky enough, we won't solve all the problems, God knows, but we'll make the world safer to go on having them.

I notice that as I get to the end of these preachments, I've started writing *we*, not *you*. This is just as well. Someday you'll do the same, as you too run out of assurances, except that the world is stranger than you imagined when you were young, as it's come to look to me. Aren't you tired of all the glib generation talk anyway? Here's another strange and wondrous element of the human condition: We overlap. Generations aren't sealed off in separate capsules. So enough about special knowledge and unique missions—ours, yours, anyone's. Enough about the vast achievements (or failings) of my generation and the unique challenges confronting yours. Each challenge is unique and each is identical—to do what's possible by finding out what's possible and, in the process, overcome what seemed possible.

Some borrowed wisdom.

From Samuel Beckett in *Worstward Ho*: "Try again. Fail again. Fail better."

From a civil rights song: "Keep your eyes on the prize, hold on."

Acknowledgments

The "Art of Mentoring" series, and this contribution to it, were the ideas of John Donatich. He, Anthony Barnett, Laurel Cook, Elinor Langer, Eric Liu, Nathan Perl-Rosenthal and Seth Colter Walls read the manuscript and advised on improvements. I did not always take their advice, but remain immensely grateful.

For many gifts, sustaining and entrancing, I am indebted to Laurel Cook.

Earlier versions of some of these pages appeared in the *Washington Post*, the *New York Times*, *Boston Review*, openDemocracy.net, *Veja*, the *Los Angeles Times*, *Mother Jones* and motherjones.com.

An Activist's Library

On the New Left of the sixties see Todd Gitlin, *The Sixties: Years of Hope, Days of Rage*; Robert Cohen and Reginald E. Zelnik, eds., *The Free Speech Movement: Reflections on Berkeley in the 1960s*; James Miller, *'Democracy Is in the Streets': From Port Huron to the Seige of Chicago*; Tom Wells, *The War Within: America's Battle over Vietnam*; Doug Rossinow, *The Politics of Authenticity: Liberalism, Christianity, and the New Left in America*; Terry H. Anderson, *The Movement and the Sixties: Protest in America from Greensboro to Wounded Knee*; and Maurice Isserman and Michael Kazin, *America Divided: The Civil War of the 1960s*.

On the civil rights movement see Clayborne Carson, *In Struggle: SNCC and the Black Awakening of the 1960s*; Aldon Morris, *The Origins of the Civil Rights Movement: Black Communities Organizing for Change*; Taylor Branch, *Parting the Waters: America in the King Years, 1954–63*; idem, *Pillar of Fire: America in the King Years, 1963–65*; and Doug McAdam, *Political Process and the Development of Black Insurgency, 1930–1970*.

On the women's movement see Ruth Rosen, *The World Split Open: How the Modern Women's Movement Changed Amer-*

ica; and Constance Curry, ed., *Deep in Our Hearts: Nine White Women in the Freedom Movement.*

On the Black Panther Party see Hugh Pearson, *The Shadow of the Panther: Huey Newton and the Price of Black Power in America.*

On the right wing see Rebecca E. Klatch, *A Generation Divided: The New Left, the New Right, and the 1960s*; Lisa McGirr, *Suburban Warriors: The Origins of the New American Right*; Rick Perlstein, *Before the Storm: Barry Goldwater and the Unmaking of the American Consensus*; and David Brock, *Blinded by the Right: The Conscience of an Ex-Conservative.*

On movements and media see Todd Gitlin, *The Whole World Is Watching: Mass Media in the Making and Unmaking of the New Left*; and Charlotte Ryan, *Prime Time Activism: Media Strategies for Organizing.*

For reconsiderations see Stephen Macedo, ed., *Rethinking the Sixties*, especially the articles by Harvey Mansfield, Jeremy Rabkin and Randall Kennedy; Todd Gitlin, *The Twilight of Common Dreams: Why America Is Wracked by Culture Wars*; and Kevin Mattson, *Intellectuals in Action: The Origins of the New Left and Radical Liberalism, 1945–1970.*

Max Weber's classic lecture "Politics as a Vocation" is available in Hans Gerth and C. Wright Mills, eds., *From Max Weber*, and on the web at www2.pfeiffer.edu/~lridener/DSS/Weber/polvoc.html.

On the humanist underpinnings of direct action there is no better primer than Albert Camus' *The Rebel.*